Six Steps to Better Thinking

How to Disagree and Get Along

Dr. Christopher DiCarlo

Suite 300 - 990 Fort St
Victoria, BC, v8v 3K2
Canada

www.friesenpress.com

Copyright © 2017 by Christopher DiCarlo
First Edition — 2017

All rights reserved.

No part of this publication may be reproduced in any form, or by any means, electronic or mechanical, including photocopying, recording, or any information browsing, storage, or retrieval system, without permission in writing from FriesenPress.

ISBN
978-1-5255-0661-1 (Hardcover)
978-1-5255-0662-8 (Paperback)
978-1-5255-0663-5 (eBook)

1. SELF-HELP

Distributed to the trade by The Ingram Book Company

It is the mark of an educated mind to be able to entertain a thought without accepting it.

– Aristotle

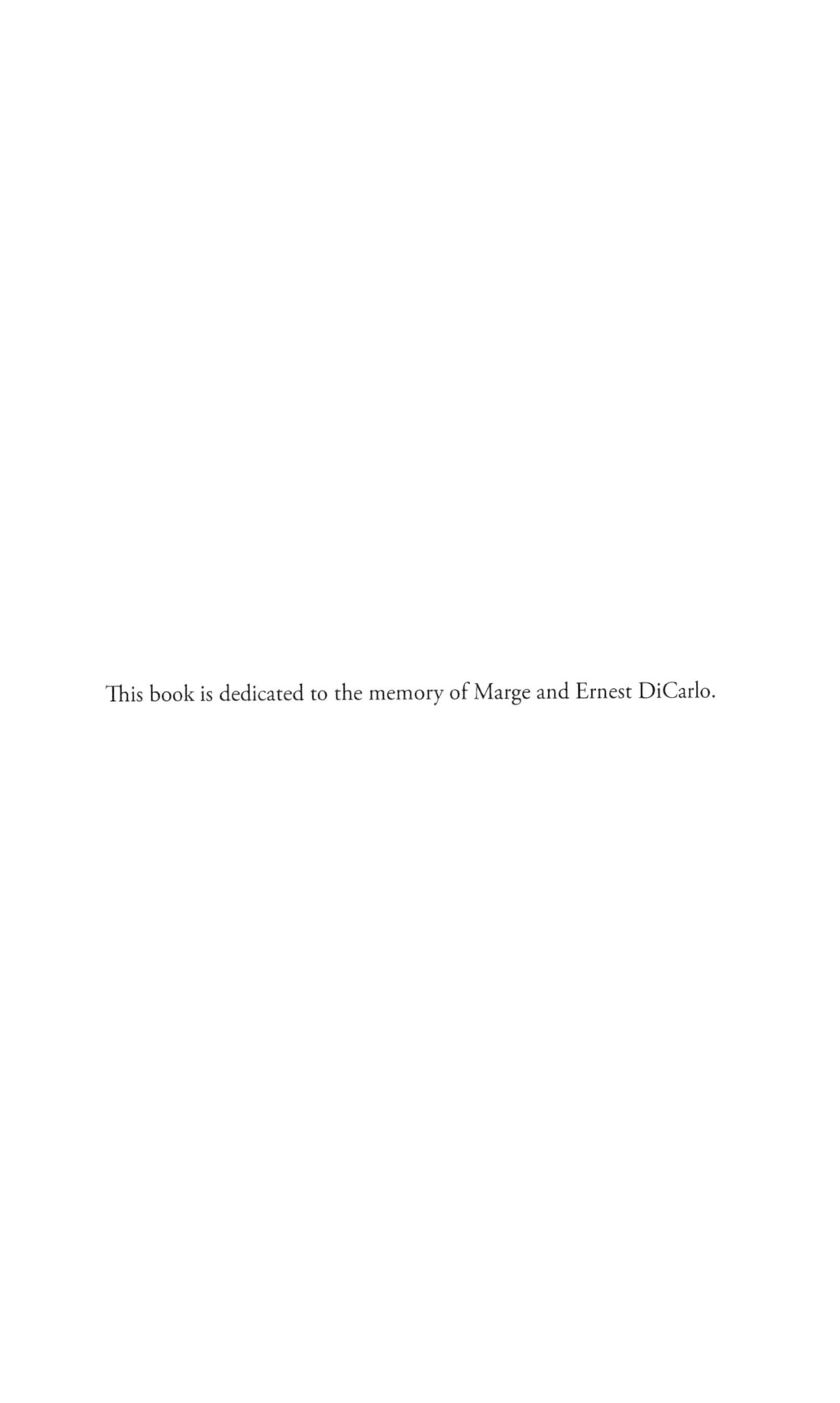

This book is dedicated to the memory of Marge and Ernest DiCarlo.

Acknowledgements

There are many people and institutions for which I am grateful in the writing of this book. I would like to thank my past professors – especially people like Jakob Amstutz at the University of Guelph whose discussion of Plato's *Apology* single-handedly convinced me to change my undergraduate major from English to Philosophy. He, along with other professors at Guelph such as Jay Newman, Doug Odegard, Helier Robinson, and Michael Ruse made my learning experiences joyful, troubling, and without end. The same holds true for my doctoral years at the University of Waterloo. People like Jan Narveson, Bill Abbott, Rolf George, Don Roberts, Joe Novak, and my co-supervisors: Jim Van Evra and Michael Ruse demonstrated considerable patience and insight during this time. As well, I am grateful for the guidance and acceptance I received during my postdoctoral work in the Stone Age Laboratory at Harvard University. My host, Ofer Bar-Yosef, was always welcoming and gracious to me as well as my family. I thank David Pilbeam, Richard Wrangham, Brian Hare, and Steven Pinker, for taking the time to have valuable discussions with me regarding cognitive evolution and human and animal reasoning. I must thank the thousands of students over the years whose inquisitiveness, sharpness, and intelligence have kept me accountable for my biases. I would also like to thank many friends and acquaintances whose good company, insights, and intelligence have nurtured my outlook on life and restored my faith in humanity. A special nod goes out to the boys in Mink's hut at the 14 ½ M Street Debating Society; this good-natured forum has allowed for the development of ideas in ways no academic institution could have provided. I would like to thank the illustrator of this book – Heather Thomson – who has done a magnificent job not only with the quality of the illustrations, but in delivering them at record speed. And to my friend and journalist, Troy Bridgeman, I thank you for the time and devotion you have made and continue to make for responsible journalism and the teaching of Critical Thinking. A special thank you goes out to Karam Singh and his lovely wife, Kuldip, who have provided both encouragement and nourishment from their wonderful Bombay Café restaurant in Guelph. And to the wait staff and many regular patrons at the Albion Hotel in downtown Guelph – Tuesday and Friday evenings would not be the same without you. And finally, a great deal of thanks is owed to my family – both extended and nuclear. My dearly departed parents, Marjory and Ernest DiCarlo, for whom this book is dedicated, have influenced me in so many ways. Their thoughtful guidance, patience, and respect have directed my understanding of the world in ways I am only now beginning to fathom. To my siblings, Brad, Marti, and Mark, and to all of their wonderful spouses and offspring, I am grateful for so many chances in which to practice what is contained in these pages. As for my wife, Linda, who has supported me in so many ways, it would be difficult to imagine my life without her encouragement, candor, and discipline. I must also thank our sons Jeremy and Matthew who have taught me more about life and what it means to be a critical thinker and a good person than all the books I could have ever read or written. And lastly, I wish to thank our dog, Pyrrho, for teaching me patience, compassion, and for keeping me young at heart. Who's a good boy? Pyrrho's a good boy!

Table of Contents

Acknowledgements ix

Introduction 3
    The Big Take Away:
    Have Meaningful Discussions, Disagree, and Get Along   6

Step 1: A is for Argument 9
    What's your point?   9
    An Argument is Like a House   10
    An Argument's Criteria is the Foundation   11
    Types of Consistency   15
    Types of Reasoning   19
        (i) Deductive Reasoning   19
        (ii) Inductive Reasoning   22
        (iii) Abductive Reasoning   23

Step 2: B is for Biases. 27
    Biological Biases   27
        (i) Genetic Influences   27
        (ii) Epigenetics   28
        (iii) Neuropsychological Influences   29
        (iv) Emotions   30
        (v) Age, Health, and Sex   32

Cultural Biases	34
(i) Family Upbringing	34
(ii) Ethnicity	35
(iii) Religion	36
(iv) Geographic Location	37
(v) Education	38
(vi) Friends	39
(vii) Media	40
(viii) Bias Check: Biases are Filters of Information	41
Bias Check	43
Biological Biases:	43
Social Biases:	43
Confirmation Bias, Fairness, and Getting Along	44

Step 3: C is for Context 47

A Cautionary Device for Considering Context	52

Step 4: D is for Diagram 55

Conclusion-Indicators	59
Premise-Indicators	59
Formal Guidelines for Diagramming a Written Argument	60
Complex Arguments	62
Legend	64

Step 5: E is for Evidence 67

Evidence and Assumptions	68
Anecdotal Evidence	69
Legal Evidence	70
Intuition	71

Scientific Evidence	72
The Scientific Method	72
Scientific Studies	77

Step 6: F is for Fallacies 81

Ad Hominem	82
Ad Ignorantiam	85
Appeal to Authority	86
Ad Populum or Appeal to Popularity	87
Begging the Question	88
Disanalogy	90
Equivocation	91
False Dilemma	93
Hasty Generalization	95
Post Hoc Fallacy	97
Red Herring	100
The Slippery Slope Fallacy	103
Strawman Fallacy	105

How to Disagree and Get Along 107

Discussing Controversial Issues: Disagreeing and Getting Along	110
(i) Euthanasia: Physician Assisted Dying (PAD) or Medical Assistance in Dying (MAID)l - For/Against	111
Common Ground	112
(ii) Abortion: Pro-Choice versus Pro-Life	113
Common Ground	116
(iii) Gun Control - For/Against	117
Common Ground	118

(iv) Capital Punishment - For/Against	119
Common Ground	120
(v) Same-Sex Relationships	
– Liberal versus Conservative	121
Common Ground	122
(vi) God/Religion – Theist versus Atheist	124
Common Ground	125

Epilogue... 127

Six Steps to Better Thinking: How to Disagree and Get Along

Introduction

The book is called what it is because there really are better and worse ways to think about things. And it really is possible to have heated discussions, disagree entirely, and still be able to get along. Due to events involving the Brexit referendum in the UK *and* the presidential elections in the U.S., the Oxford Dictionary's Word of the Year for 2016 was "post-truth" – an adjective defined as "relating to or denoting circumstances in which objective facts are less influential in shaping public opinion than appeals to emotion and personal belief."[1] This is an extremely sad commentary on how information is delivered, interpreted, and acted upon. By repeatedly stating talking points – even if they involved false information – some candidates said whatever they *felt* was appropriate to make their point. This was done through the excessive use of "echo chambers" – a media term indicating the uncritical way in which unchecked and untrue information can be repeatedly stated over and over again until it appears to be factual. In many cases, the false information is treated as factual by some news agencies. This is hauntingly similar to what Joseph Goebbels – the Reich Minister of Propaganda for the Nazis – said during World War II:

> If you tell a lie big enough and keep repeating it, people will eventually come to believe it. The lie can be maintained only for such time as the State can shield the people from the political, economic and/or military consequences of the lie. It thus becomes vitally important for the State to use all of its powers to repress dissent, for the truth is the mortal

---

1 https://en.oxforddictionaries.com/word-of-the-year/word-of-the-year-2016

enemy of the lie, and thus by extension, the truth is the greatest enemy of the State.[2]

Once "fake news" becomes accepted as factual, it feeds on confirmation bias and becomes entrenched in the minds of people who *want* to believe it to be true. However, in attempting to respond to and correct the falsities, those who wish to fact check such claims often come under attack as belonging to a grand conspiracy, trying to suppress the truth. Post-truth politics makes considerable use of conspiracy theories. To further criticize such conspiracy theories with things like facts is to be a member of the "mainstream media" or "The Establishment". In critical thinking, this is called "insulating one's argument against criticism". It is an attempt to make any claim impervious to scrutiny and criticism. And we will have none of that in this book, and hopefully, in society. In order to live in free and just societies, all information is open to criticism and scrutiny without exception. And so it's time to make facts and critical thinking sexy again.

It has unfortunately become quite fashionable today to claim that what people *feel* about issues should be taken as seriously as the facts about those issues. Emotional attachment to specific viewpoints and the facts about the world are often two completely different things. It's not as though a person's feelings are not to be validated; they are. However, one's feelings should only be validated up and until the point where they conflict with the facts.

Phrases like "there are better and worse ways to think about things" and "six steps to better thinking" imply that there is value to our beliefs, our ideas, and our opinions. And that some ideas are better than others. But what makes these objects of the mind and influencers of behavior good, bad, better, or worse? How are they measured? Who determines the value of our beliefs? Luckily, much of the hard work has already been done. Philosophers, mathematicians, logicians, scientists, writers, and many others have developed the critical-thinking skills that require all of us to make such valued distinctions. I have taken these skills and distilled them into six easy-to-remember steps.

---

2 From the Jewish Virtual Library: http://www.jewishvirtuallibrary.org/jsource/Holocaust/goebbelslie.html

It is by no means an accident that each of the six steps (or skills) corresponds to the first six letters of the English alphabet.

Step 1: A is for Argument
Step 2: B is for Bias
Step 3: C is for Context
Step 4: D is for Diagram
Step 5: E is for Evidence
Step 6: F is for Fallacies

In this way, the letters act as a handy mnemonic. Remember the letters and you can more easily remember and apply the most basic steps for becoming a better thinker. Combined, these steps form a skill set that will allow anyone greater capacity to have more meaningful discussions about all issues – from the simple to the sublime. In other words, this is a book that quickly teaches people *how* to think. *What* you think is up to you, but there are specific rules that govern better and worse *ways* of thinking. And we shall go through them one step at a time.

At this point, you may be asking yourself why these particular six steps are valuable, and in what ways they will make you a *better* thinker.

You will be a better thinker after learning these six steps, because you will more effectively communicate *what* it is that you believe and *why* it is you believe it, so that people will have an easier time understanding you. As well, because of these six steps, you will be empowered with the capacity to better understand what people are saying to you and to know the various components of why and what it is they are saying. Your thinking will become better as well, because what emerges from your ability to understand and use these skills is an element of diplomacy and fairness when having discussions and dialogue about important issues. And this will translate into more civil disagreement.

The Big Take Away: Have Meaningful Discussions, Disagree, and Get Along

The biggest take away from this book is that, if people use the six steps *fairly*, they will be more empowered to have meaningful discussions about important issues, disagree entirely, and still be able to get along. Learning these skills will allow us to value discourse over hatred, dialogue over violence, and most importantly, fairness and understanding in our disagreements on important issues.

> The concept of *Fairness* is the *Golden Rule of Dialogue* and the *Cornerstone of Critical Thinking*.

If we play fairly, and the others with whom we disagree play fairly, I will guarantee you that both sides will get the most of what they want. But – and this is a *very big* but – both sides *must* play fairly for this to work. If this were done more often, it would save untold amounts of time, energy, and money. But we can be greedy, self-centered, and stupid. And in so doing, can decide not to play fairly. There are few values we humans hold dearer than fairness. We have built-in fairness detectors within us. And as such, when it comes to decisions and judgments, we tend to dispute results less if we believe that they were at least arrived at in a fair and just manner. So if we can be fair even when disagreeing, it will increase our capacity to understand differences of opinions. And in a world where disagreements are going to happen, we need to re-learn how to have important discussions, which may become emotionally heated, but also realize that we can and should still get along. It's *easy* to agree and get along. But we have forgotten how to value and use the art of disagreement in civil and political discourse. It is important for us to know that it's *okay* to disagree. We need to accept that we're not always going to agree. And that it's *okay* to be diametrically opposed to another's viewpoints and still be their neighbor, friend, in-law, co-worker, or family member.

You believe in God; she doesn't. You believe the Republican or Conservative political philosophy is superior; he thinks the Democrats or Liberals know better. You like the Red Sox; she likes the Yankees. You're pro-life; she's pro-choice. You say, "To-mah-to"; she says: "Shut the f#*k up!"[3]

The big take away here is that we need to re-learn how to disagree and still get along, and this requires maturity and diplomacy, but above all else, it requires *fairness*. And these are not easy traits to develop. In fact, developing and practicing them is one of the toughest challenges we face as inhabitants of a civilized world. Thankfully, the skills of critical thinking provide us with the capacity to be mature, diplomatic, and fair, and allow us to disagree in a civil manner. For the majority of us, developing such skills will not happen overnight ... or in a week, or a month. It is something that is ongoing and requires continuous practice, development, and use. But this takes time and a lot of practice. And in today's age of immediacy, with information and opinion just a click away, there seems to be less and less time in which to practice such skills. Perhaps this is one of the reasons so many people are feeling their way through issues rather than thinking critically about them.

---

[3] This joke has been said by a lot of comedians. I'm going to nod my head in the direction of Dennis Miller for this one.

Step 1: A is for Argument

<u>What's your point?</u>

If you want someone to understand what you are saying, then you need to learn how to put your ideas into the forms of arguments. To state your point clearly, you must understand some basic rules. First of all, every argument is made up of two parts: a main point and the reasons for believing the main point. Your main point is formally called a *conclusion*. And the reasons for believing your main point are called *premises*. An argument is the way you put together or structure your ideas, opinions, or beliefs so that people will better understand what it is that you are trying to say.

Premise(s) + Conclusion = Argument

Consider whether or not you believe any of the following statements to be true:

-Men are generally physically stronger than women.
-The world is flat.
-Justin Bieber is the greatest entertainer of all time.
-Albany is the capital of New York State.
-The moon landing was a hoax.

-9/11 was not caused by Islamo-terrorists.
-Democracy is the greatest political system ever developed.
-Vaccines cause autism.
-2 + 2 = 4.

In order to comment on these conclusions with a 'yes' or 'no' response, you would need to provide reasons or premises in order to state your main point as an argument. Why, for example, would you believe that Justin Bieber is the greatest entertainer of all time? Especially since we really know it's Kanye. Just kidding. If you ask me, it's neither. And I have my reasons. Or premises. And you need to think about yours every time you make a claim about something or someone, or some policy or law, or someone's hairstyle, or whatever.

An Argument is Like a House

When it comes to arguments, you need to think of a house. Your conclusion is the roof. Your walls are the premises. And your foundation is made up of universal criteria.

Your roof (conclusion) may be a relatively innocuous claim: "It's a lovely day today." Or it could be more controversial: "Elvis was abducted by aliens." But there is a general rule: The greater the conclusion (roof), the stronger the premises (walls) need to be.

All houses (as arguments) must rest upon the same foundations (universal criteria). However, not all arguments abide by these criteria as well as others. And so their premises (walls) become weakened and prone to imbalance. If premises can be demonstrated to be weak in some respects, the house (argument) becomes increasingly prone to collapse.

Not all of our arguments will be able to stand under scrutiny. This is simply a fact of life. For those of you who thought you had good reasons or premises to believe that Santa Claus existed (SPOILER ALERT), and then found out he didn't (TOO LATE), do you still believe in him? Of course not. Your conclusion could not withstand the scrutiny of critical thinking. But that's okay. Many of our beliefs come under similar scrutiny and must suffer the same fate. And if we are wise, we emerge from the rubble of these fallen houses with the renewed ambition to start building new houses with stronger walls.

An Argument's Criteria is the Foundation

In order for an argument to be solid, not only must the walls be sturdy but the foundation must provide the greatest support. There are several universal criteria that make up the foundation. In critical thinking, criteria are really just standards of judgment that we use for evaluating or testing our claims and those of others. Fortunately, there is universal agreement about the criteria used to support the evidence of our premises, which effectively and efficiently allows us to speak to one another on a fairly level playing field.

The greatest of all universal criteria in critical thinking is *consistency*. If an argument is not consistent, it is weak and extremely prone to collapse. Consistency is so important that it is sometimes referred to as "the mother of all criteria" and the guiding principle of rational behavior. Aside from a few world leaders, can you think of a time when *anyone* was ever praised – either in speech or in action – for their inconsistencies? We tend to dislike inconsistencies, because we understand the world best when we can predict (with some accuracy) the anticipated outcomes of actions. When our expectations are violated, we experience a sense of dissonance, and identify (on a very pragmatic level) the negative aspects and consequences of such inconsistencies. All species highly value consistency in communication and action. This is what I believe to be one of the main reasons why humans and other species universally place so much value on the criterion of consistency. Recognizing and utilizing that future events will be similar to past events involves inductive and comparative reasoning, and it has been hardwired into us. Because if our beliefs and actions are inconsistent to the way the world actually works, it often has very drastic and harmful effects. If you think that you can fly like a bird simply by flapping your arms, gravity is going to teach you a very painful lesson. So should you have such an inconsistent belief, I suggest that you attempt your flight from the ground, rather than a rooftop or cliff. In this way, nature will quickly demonstrate to you the inconsistency of your belief, without all the injuries, pain, or death.

In an alternate Trump universe, with alternative facts, post-truth politics, etc., there is a great need for clarity of thought, empowerment in presentation of ideas, and directness in communication. People need to know not only when they're being lied to, or presented with alternative facts, or double-spoken to in a hauntingly similar manner to that found in Orwell's *1984*; people need to be able to call it what it is: bullshit! And they need to be able to understand the nuances and the qualities of such statements in order to hold others accountable for their beliefs and their actions.

The great ancient Greek philosopher, Aristotle, decided there had to be a foundational logic that could cut through this kind of bamboozery and hucksterism which defied consistency. And so he developed some basic principles of classical logic known as the Three Laws of Thought. Each law provides the basis for the power and effectiveness of the criterion of consistency:

(i) The Law of Identity

This is the first and most basic law. It states that: 'x = x' where x refers in both cases to the same thing at the same time and in the same respect. The truth of this law becomes obvious whenever someone tries to make statements such as: "A car is not a car" or "A grizzly bear is a paper airplane". Violating such a law immediately reveals an inconsistency i.e. don't try to fold up and fly a grizzly bear.

Some proper examples of such a law include:

Raymond is bald	=	Raymond has no hair
Sweden has witnessed Peace for over 50 years	=	Sweden has not been at war for over half a century
The current temperature is 32° Fahrenheit	=	The current temperature is 0° Celsius

This law provides a basis for us to understand what things are by what defines them, as well as how they are distinguished from everything else. This law also helps to provide order and consistency in our world. Imagine a world in which people, statements, and objects randomly changed properties and functions. For example, if you tried to drive your car but it changed into a ten-foot banana, or on some days, it rained water, on other days, it rained Skittles; or gravity randomly reversed its pull, neither you, nor anyone else, nor any other species on this planet, would be able to predict and exercise any type of control over their environments. So we should probably be a little more thankful to Aristotle for establishing some of the anchors of consistency.

(ii) The Law of Non-Contradiction

This law maintains that either a state of being or a statement and its negation cannot both be true. In other words, it is impossible – both logically and physically – for an object to be entirely red and entirely green at the same time and in the same respect. It is impossible for me to be both hopping on one leg and not hopping on one leg at the same time and in the same respect. In the same manner, we can also say that a statement cannot both be true and false simultaneously. For example, the statement: 'The Toronto Blue Jays won the 1993 World Series *and* they lost it', is a contradictory statement and cannot be true. The law is basically saying: "You can't have your cake and eat it too."

(iii) The Law of Excluded Middle

This law states that any state of being or any meaningful claim must either be true or false. For example, it must either be true or false that you can walk 500 miles in a single day or not. And we all know that there's no such thing as being a little bit pregnant. With this law, there is literally no middle ground. It is a binary law. It is disjunctive i.e. it states that either something is true or it's not.

Combined, we use the three laws of thought in everyday discussions as well as in the most detailed and heated debates. They are foundational to our understanding of the importance of consistency as a criterion to which our premises should adhere.

These laws are considered the foundations of rational thought because they disallow people from stating unaccountable inconsistencies and contradictions. So, for example, when the newly inaugurated President of the United States, Donald Trump, boldly proclaimed that the pictures of crowds at his inauguration were falsified and there were well over a million supporters in attendance; and that God stopped the skies from raining on his inauguration even though his wife is holding an umbrella and other members in the crowd (including past President George W. Bush) are all wearing plastic ponchos because it was raining; and he said the skies opened and the sun shone down on him because of God, these all violate the Three Laws of Thought which underlie the criterion of consistency. And yet, Trump is such a good marketer, it appears that he believes if he keeps telling the same lies, then to echo Goebbels, people will come to believe them. The reason why facts are important, and evidence is important, and establishing the truth is important, is because it holds people accountable who try to use pretzel logic and biased rhetoric in an attempt to circumvent the Three Laws of Thought which provide the foundational appeal of consistency to our statements. Without these laws of thought, anything goes. And such a world is far too unsettling, disturbing, and dangerous to allow this to happen. It is for these reasons and more that *consistency* is the mother of all criteria when it comes to supporting premises.

Types of Consistency

There are two types of consistency: internal and external.

Internal consistency refers to the way in which one's premises are related and consistent to each other within a particular belief system.

I can, for example, display spectacular internal consistency that demonstrates why I believe the reason my car keys go missing so often is actually due to invisible gnomes. Because they are invisible, I can never see them in the act of taking my car keys. They are extremely tricky and intelligent creatures who, in their invisibility, always manage to elude my ability to catch them in the act.

Although this argument may seem internally consistent, my conclusion and supporting premises have no *external consistency* with the natural world and our understanding of it. In the attempt to confirm such a claim, we might set up traps, motion-detecting sensors, and video-surveillance cameras, to provide the empirical evidence required for people to believe that such things as invisible gnomes truly exist. However, when no such evidence turns up, what are we to believe? The lack of evidence has falsified such a conclusion. This then leads us to maintain that, although internally consistent, this argument bears no external consistency with the natural world. And so, without supporting evidence that leads me to conclude that invisible gnomes really exist in the natural world, I am not compelled in any way to believe such an argument.

One of the quickest ways to spot inconsistency is to identify contradictions. For example, whenever someone makes a universal claim – whether affirmative (e.g. "I always do ___.") or negative (e.g., "I never do ___."), you can demonstrate inconsistency in his or her claims by providing just one counter-factual incident. Think of how many people throughout history have stood for specific values and principles – like truth, justice, freedom, and dignity – only to be discovered to violate these principles. Think of how many times communities have been shocked to discover the inconsistent behavior of their politicians, physicians, priests, coaches, bosses, teachers, and so on.

Make sure your premises are consistent. Otherwise, they will not be valued and your house will fall.

There are other universal criteria that act as foundations, upon which to anchor our premises:

Simplicity – sometimes referred to as parsimony – is universally valued as a criterion to support premises, because if we can present an argument that accomplishes just as much but with fewer premises, it tends to be more highly valued. This is known as Occam's razor. William of Occam was a 14th century Franciscan Friar and scholastic philosopher. He was best known for saying, "Do not multiply entities beyond necessity."[4] What he meant by this is that you really don't need more premises than are necessary to responsibly support your conclusion and satisfy the foundational criteria. Occam was the originator of the KISS Principle (Keep It Simple Stupid). In other words, when faced with competing arguments, the one that can say more with less is generally favored. It just makes more sense for us to believe that a less complicated and more precise manner for providing evidence of a conclusion is better than a drawn-out and complicated one. Although less is not always best, because some ideas require extremely complex arguments, for the purposes of practicality and efficiency, the criterion of simplicity is universally valued.

Another very important foundational criterion is *reliability*. The manner in which information used as premises was attained is extremely important.

---

[4] https://plato.stanford.edu/entries/ockham/#4.1

Attaining dependable factual information is critical in the continued support of one's conclusion. Reliability is a universal criterion that demands that we attain our information from trustworthy sources, and that we do not shirk our responsibility in this regard. Many U.S. voters during the 2016 election formulated opinions about whom they should vote based on information they read on Facebook or Twitter. The problem with such sources of information is that it is very easy to present "fake news". As we saw in the Introduction, if you tell a lie often enough, it will become accepted as the truth. Reliability of shared information is essential, and that is why teachers and journalists generally hold such important roles in society. If the information the public receives has not been attained in a responsible and reliable manner, then we (the people) suffer, because we are not making *informed* decisions about that information.

It follows that reliability and media literacy go hand in hand. The more literate one is in terms of reliable media sources, the greater the likelihood of stronger premises. And conversely, the more gullible one is in accepting information from dubious and unreliable sources, the greater the likelihood for weaker premises. The same holds true for the information provided by professionals within given fields. For example, an ultrasound will provide more reliable information about the development of a fetus than a psychic could. A qualified physician will be more reliable in telling you about the importance of vaccinations than a famous model/actress. And a certified, licensed garage mechanic will be more reliable in telling you information about your car than an unqualified athlete. So it follows that, if it can be demonstrated that the premises of an argument have not been attained from reliable sources, it becomes quite easy to demonstrate their weakness and topple the argument (house).

We now need to turn our attention to the foundational and universal criterion of *relevance*. It seems obvious that premises should be relevant to the conclusion. And yet there are many ways in which people can introduce irrelevant premises into an argument in the guise of presenting relevant points. The fallacy called a "red herring" is a fallacy of improper relevance. Many Red Herring Fallacies were committed during the September 27, 2016 presidential debate, by both Donald Trump and Hilary Clinton.

When asked how he was going to cut taxes for the wealthy, Donald Trump said, "Well, I'm really calling for major jobs, because the wealthy are going to cause tremendous jobs." When asked specifically about her tax-increase proposals, Hilary Clinton criticized Trump's ideas rather than stipulate, specifically, what her own plan was to address this issue. Remember, a conclusion should follow from the premises supplied, and if they are relevant, they will provide the conclusion with greater support. When your premises are irrelevant, they don't count – for anything. So stick to the topic!

The next universal criterion to consider is *sufficiency*. We all have some idea of what it means for something to be sufficient. Sufficiency requires enough of *something* to satisfy some condition, want, goal, etc. For example, if I am hoping to get a Lamborghini for my eighteenth birthday, but more importantly, I want a car in which to drive to school, then an Elantra will actually be sufficient.

In critical thinking, we often talk of premises providing the conclusion with *enough* evidence for support. But how much is enough? When are the premises sufficient in providing enough evidence to convince someone of your conclusion? The astronomer Carl Sagan once said, "Extraordinary claims require extraordinary evidence." This basically means that the larger or more substantial your conclusion is, the more sufficiently convincing the evidence will need to be to support it. For example, if someone were to claim that Bigfoot exists, then what premises would sufficiently support this conclusion? For years, we have seen people claiming to have seen Bigfoot, found his big footy prints in snow, heard him, and so on. Many different premises have been offered, but none have been able to satisfy the foundational criterion of sufficiency. And that's because no one has ever presented compelling evidence that satisfies this criterion. But there is one very simple way to sufficiently prove Bigfoot's existence: Show us a body! That's all that needs to be done to sufficiently prove such a being exists. You would think, with so many sightings, that eventually someone, somewhere, would shoot one of these sasquatches, or stumble across the corpse of one. So far, there has been nothing but hearsay, bad video footage, ridiculous footprint casts, and legendary tales. So the argument for the existence of Bigfoot fails because it does not present sufficient premises to support such a conclusion.

These five universal criteria – consistency, simplicity, reliability, relevance, and sufficiency – provide the foundational support upon which our premises rest. If we can demonstrate that an argument's premises fail to satisfy any (or all) of these criteria, then the argument is doomed to collapse. And keep in mind that it does not matter how much one is emotionally attached to an argument. The tools of critical thinking are not concerned with how we *feel* about issues, ideas, or beliefs. In this respect, these tools are like the principles of mathematics. They are neutral and serve us only when used in accordance to their definitions and intended use.

Types of Reasoning

Now that we understand how an argument is like a house, it's time to consider the ways in which we build our arguments – our houses – as solid structures. These are called "types of reasoning" and they're really just different ways in which we can consider information. Although there are several different types or ways to reason and develop arguments, we are just going to consider the three that are arguably the most important:

Deductive Reasoning

Inductive Reasoning

Abductive Reasoning

(i) Deductive Reasoning

Deductive reasoning is the type of reasoning that readers believe Sherlock Holmes used in solving his crimes, in Arthur Conan Doyle's stories of the great detective. To carefully sift through the evidence surrounding a crime, understand the *relationship* between the various pieces, and knowing what *must* follow from the evidence – not what *might* follow or *could* follow – leads to an inevitable and definite conclusion as to the identity of the murderer. If you have ever played the board game *Clue,* you know that, once the identity of the murderer has been determined (through the process of elimination), it clearly *has* to have been that particular person, in that specific place, with that specific weapon – no *ifs, ands,* or *buts* about it. For example, *Professor Plum* did it in the *library* with a *lead pipe*. It's not as though it *may* have been him; no, no, no. It *had* to be him! The conclusion reached using deductive reasoning is certain and irreversible. The conclusion *must* follow from the premises. Formally, this is known as "logical validity".

Here are some examples of Deductive Reasoning:

- If all humans are mortal, and you are a human, then it must follow that you are mortal.

- If you are allergic to peanuts, and had eaten peanuts, you would have trouble breathing. But you are not having trouble breathing, and so it must follow that you have not eaten peanuts.

- If all squirrels have cells in their bodies, and all cells contain DNA, then it must follow that squirrels have DNA.

- If all politicians are liars, and Jones is a politician, it must follow that Jones is a liar.

- If two people are in an elevator, and one of them farts, it must follow that everyone knows who did it.

In all of the above examples, keep in mind that the premises do not necessarily have to be true for the argument to be valid. Their truth is assumed. In other words, we assume that, *if* the premises are true, the conclusion has to follow.

Here's a story that clearly illustrates the assumed truth of premises and the use of deductive reasoning:

Imagine that, in a large Midwestern U.S. town, there's a fundraising dinner in honor of a politician named Dorothy Shaw. Ms. Shaw is running for re-election as senator of a Midwestern state, but she is late arriving at the gala dinner. The master of ceremonies is worried and so asks Father Bennett – a Catholic priest, who was seated at the head table – to get up and talk to the audience until Ms. Shaw arrives. He agrees to do so and says the following:

"When I was first ordained as a priest, quite a few years ago, I was given the task of hearing confession.[5] You can imagine how shocked I was when my first confessor was a woman who confessed to me that she had poisoned her husband's tea. The poison caused her husband to have a heart attack and he died. She then confessed to having received one million dollars in insurance money for his death!"

At that particular moment, Senator Shaw arrives and the crowd applauds. Father Bennett joins the applause as he returns to his seat. The senator makes her way to the podium. After the applause quiets, she thanks everybody for attending, looks at the head table, and recognizes Father Bennett. "Well it certainly is good to see everyone here tonight. Thank you all for coming. I see that Father Bennett is here. Father Bennett might not realize this, but I was his first confessor."

She wonders why an awkward silence falls over the room.

Now, what can we conclude – or more accurately, deduce – from these premises? Is it that Dorothy Shaw poisoned her husband's tea, killed him, and collected one million dollars in insurance money? You could answer yes, no, or maybe. Given the information we have at this point in time, the correct answer in this case is 'maybe'. We do not actually have all the facts, and so we cannot know for sure if Dorothy Shaw is a murderer. However, here is how deductive reasoning works. *If* what Father Bennett said is true, and *if* what Dorothy Shaw said is true, it *must* follow that she poisoned her husband's tea, causing him to have a heart attack and thereby killing him, and then collected one million dollars in insurance money. But notice that the premises *must* be true in order for the conclusion to follow. This is how deductive reasoning works. The conclusion *must* follow from the previous premises. In other words, it cannot be otherwise.

---

[5] For those unfamiliar with Catholicism, confession is an action that takes place between a parishioner of the Catholic faith and a priest. The parishioner confesses their sins in what is called a confessional – a type of booth within a church where the identity of the parishioner is kept secret from the priest. The priest then offers forgiveness and the person often must do a type of penance in order to be forgiven for sinning.

But remember: the conclusion that Dorothy Shaw is a murderer can only follow *if* what both she and Father Bennett said are true. Father Bennett could have been mistaken. Perhaps it was his third confessor who confessed to being a murderer and not his first. Or perhaps Ms. Shaw was mistaken and was not actually his first confessor. If we investigated further, we could establish Dorothy's innocence by discovering that her husband is still alive. Or that she never married. Then these findings would immediately exonerate her from the charge of murder. But never forget, with deductive reasoning, *if* what she said is true, and *if* what Father Bennett said is true, then she *must* be a murderer. Just like in the game of *Clue*, there can be no other way about it. Deductive reasoning is a very powerful tool in formulating arguments and understanding the inferences of premises.

(ii) Inductive Reasoning

Unlike deductive reasoning, the conclusions arrived at using inductive reasoning are not logically valid, but are considered to be warranted, reasonable, or probable. With deductive reasoning, we know that, if the premises are assumed to be true and follow specific forms, then the conclusion must logically follow. With inductive reasoning, human observations provide probable conclusions through the use of statistical generalizations. This would be an example: If I hold a pen between two fingers and then open them, you would watch the pen fall to the table. If I were to do this repeatedly, there would accumulate sufficient statistical instances to warrant the generalization that the next time I open my fingers, the pen will fall to the table. This is how inductive reasoning works. It is the hallmark of scientific reasoning. It allows us to generalize that future episodes will be similar to past episodes. It is by no means a perfect type of reasoning, but it is nonetheless a very powerful tool in understanding cause-and-effect relationships in the natural world. This type of reasoning has allowed scientists to put people on the moon, cure diseases, circumnavigate the globe, and all and every other manner of scientific discovery.

(iii) Abductive Reasoning

Unlike either deductive or inductive reasoning, abductive reasoning is interesting and unique. It is sometimes referred to as "reasoning to the best explanation". And what that means is that when there isn't enough evidence to definitively conclude and understand a particular aspect of the world, abductive reasoning is often used to provide a hypothesis that makes sense for now. An historical example should illustrate this type of reasoning quite well: In Vienna, Austria in the 1840s, there was a physician named Dr. Ignaz Semmelweis. In the hospital at which Dr. Semmelweis worked, women in his ward were dying of what was called "childbed fever".

Dr. Ignaz Semmelweis

The death rate in his ward was roughly five times higher than in the other wards, where women were tended to by midwives. He was perplexed that this was happening, since great care had been taken to assure that women in his ward would not be afflicted with such a deadly illness.

Here's a bit of a back story: During that time in history, no women were admitted to medical school. The male medical students would first go to anatomy class and then to the various wards to examine patients. They did not wash their hands, wear gloves, or use any disinfectant whatsoever, because no germ theory existed at that time. One day, Semmelweis observed his friend and colleague working on a cadaver who had accidentally cut himself with a scalpel. A few days later, the man died exhibiting the exact same symptoms as the women who were dying of childbed fever. Semmelweis realized that there must be something in the cadavers that was being passed along to the women and caused their illness. He hypothesized that such 'cadaveric matter' might be too small for the naked eye to see. So he had all of the medical students wash their hands in chlorinated lime before they visited the wards. The number of incidences of childbed fever dropped dramatically. Even though Semmelweis could not see the germs that were causing the illness, he hypothesized that such microscopic agents *must* be the cause of the illness. And so he could confirm his hypothesis by using a strong antibacterial cleansing agent. This is how Semmelweis reasoned abductively to the best explanation of the cause of childbed fever. Sadly, history is not without irony. Even though Semmelweis correctly used abductive reasoning to save so many lives, his professional peers scoffed at his germ theory hypothesis and refused to listen to him. He was fired from the hospital and spent his final days attempting to popularize his book: *The Etiology, Concept, and Prophylaxis of Childbed Fever*. His professional colleagues rejected his views and he eventually suffered from depression, forgetfulness, and other neurological complaints (possibly Alzheimer's disease or early onset dementia). He was admitted to a mental asylum where he was kicked and beaten by staff. His wounds became infected; and he died of sepsis – the very type of infection his abductive reasoning cured in so many women. Fortunately, for the rest of humanity, his ideas were eventually taken seriously by scientists such as Louis Pasteur and Joseph Lister and were adopted by the entire medical community. Today, we owe much to this man and his use of abductive reasoning.

A is for Argument. It is important to remember that an argument takes the form of a house with its conclusion as the roof, its premises as the walls, and the universal criteria as the foundation. When it comes to the types of reasoning used in argumentation, we have considered three types: deduction, induction, and abduction.

Now that we have considered some of the basic key components of arguments in step one, we need to turn our attention in step two towards the various factors that cause us to see and understand the world differently from one another, and that lead to disagreements. These are called "biases".

Step 2: B is for Biases

A bias is a way in which people are influenced or constrained in the various ways they understand and act upon various types of information. The manner in which we eventually come to acquire, revise, and retain opinions, beliefs, and attitudes about issues is the result of a long process of development, influenced by internal and external biases. Even before we were born, there were factors that would influence and bias the way in which we see and understand the world. We now need to become familiar with what these factors are in order to better understand how and why we now believe the things we do. There are many different types of biases. But they all generally fall under two categories: *biological* and *cultural*.

Biological Biases

(i) Genetic Influences

The DNA in our body codes for particular types of traits and behaviors, just as it does in every other living plant and animal species on the planet. It should come as little surprise then that our own genetic makeup will bias us in particular ways. For example, just consider the characteristic traits of homosexuality and attention deficit hyperactive disorder (ADHD). If you believe that homosexuality is a life choice, and has no basis in biology, then explain why homosexuals, throughout the ages, didn't simply choose not to be so. They have suffered and been oppressed for millennia because of sexual attraction beyond their choosing. We need to better understand how sexual orientation is biased in biology. This would allow us to treat people more fairly and equitably. But it requires the acknowledgment and understanding of the biological sciences as they relate to human sexuality. We shall consider this topic in more depth in the final chapter. For now, we need to realize that the same biological constraints that hold true for heterosexuals hold true in biasing people to be homosexual. People are biologically biased to be attracted to the opposite sex, the same sex, animals, vegetables, and all manner of inanimate objects. And yes, as difficult as this will be for some to accept, we must even realize that pedophiles are biased to be attracted to children.

A similar type of biological bias holds true for those afflicted with ADHD. Before the development of a genetic understanding of human behavior, young students afflicted with the genes for ADHD faced great difficulty and challenges, not to mention ridicule and punishment from their teachers, parents, and others. Now that we know far more about the genetic factors that bias someone toward ADHD, we are in a better position to understand how people with this particular bias behave, and in so doing, can more efficiently facilitate an environment in which they may thrive, contribute, and excel.

(ii) Epigenetics

Keep in mind that genes do not work solely in isolation, but in relation to other genes and environmental factors. The field of epigenetics is advancing in ways that demonstrate how environmental factors play a key role in influencing the ways genes either express or do not express under specific circumstances. Epigenetics literally means "on top of" or "above" genetics. So modifications to DNA occur externally, which either slows or speeds up the process of turning genes on or keeping them suppressed. The modifications themselves do not change or alter the DNA sequence. Instead, they affect how cells *read* genes. An analogy for epigenetics that is sometimes used to clarify matters compares a person's DNA to the script of a movie. The lines of the actors would direct conversation within the shooting of the film as genes do within our bodies. However, epigenetics act like the director of the film. And different directors would create different ways in how the movie would appear and play out.[6]

One of the more striking examples of epigenetics involves the use of mice models. Chronic stress, due to separation from their mothers experienced early in life, has altered not only the adult behavior of mice but also their offspring for several generations. Even though the offspring had not undergone the same stress conditions as their parents or grandparents, they still experience the same depressive and impulsive behaviors and altered social skills. In other words, some of the actions and behavior of your grandparents will influence the speed and frequency in which your genes either express or do not express for particular traits. This particular bias is completely beyond your control and comes from past generations. Not to freak you out or anything, but one can only imagine what we are currently doing in our lives that may have similar effects on our grandchildren in the future.

(iii) Neuropsychological Influences

Because brain activity is at the seat of how we process information, we need to seriously consider how it may bias or influence our behavior. If you've ever known anyone who has suffered with mental illness, you will understand the ways in which they are biased to see the world differently, simply because there may be a chemical imbalance within their brains. Psychological disorders such as depression and schizophrenia can have devastating effects on people and their families. We are led to conclude then that the minds of those who suffer from mental illness are biased in ways that make specific actions beyond their control.

Anyone who happens to possess a gene that diminishes the amount of the neurotransmitter serotonin in their brain is likely to act extremely impulsively

---

6 See: http://www.whatisepigenetics.com/what-is-epigenetics/

under certain conditions. And this could, under the right circumstances, lead to further problems, such as criminal behavior. Others will have the misfortune of possessing genes that increase the neural-chemical reactions that foster a greater likelihood for addiction. A person such as myself, who does not consume alcohol at all because I do not like the taste, must possess a type of brain that, for some reason, allows me to abstain from enjoying and thereby craving the consumption of alcohol. We can now ask ourselves what the difference might be between my brain and the brain of an alcoholic. How are we biased differently in these respects? His entire life will be affected because of liquids that contain alcohol, whereas my life is entirely unaffected by such beverages.

This does not mean that we can never alter or modify our current behavior. There are plenty of programs that deal with addictive behavior. So we have the ability to change or modify our biases when we recognize how they may interfere negatively with our lives. However, the point to note here is that some people will simply be more biologically prone to such biases than others. But even though this may be the case, our lot in life is not set completely in stone. Current research into the neuroplasticity of our brains indicate that the brain has the ability to re-wire itself, so that the neural signals do not continue to follow pathways that cause human behavior to follow similar patterns. For example, people who suffer from Obsessive Compulsive Disorder (OCD) can alter the old ways their brains were accustomed to working. In this way, we can understand how our brains are more *plastic* or flexible. Through specific training techniques, people have been able to overcome Post Traumatic Stress Disorders (PTSD), Obsessive Compulsive Disorders (OCD), and some success has been reported in the treatment of schizophrenia using neural re-circuitry techniques. These are but a few of the many ways neuropsychological factors can deeply bias, influence, and affect our beliefs and actions.

(iv) Emotions

Emotions can be defined as affective states – such as fear, anger, sorrow, joy, disgust, anticipation, surprise – which can motivate human behavior.

There are also more subtle variations such as terror or phobia, rage, sadness, grief, depression, happiness, etc. These emotional states are cross-culturally universal. That means, no matter where we travel in the world, we can all recognize when someone is happy, sad, angry, afraid, surprised, etc. But what causes emotional states? And why do we so often find humans at the mercy of them? To answer this, it is important to remember that, as humans, we were emotional beings long before we were rational beings. The parts of our brain responsible for our emotional states are located in the center of our brain and are known collectively as the limbic system. The part of our brain responsible for rational decision-making is often attributed to the prefrontal cerebral cortex. In terms of cognitive evolution, that is to say, how and when our brains developed, cognitive scientists believe that the limbic system is much older than the recently developed prefrontal cortex. And so it should not be surprising then that we often react to information emotionally first and then must think rationally about it afterwards. One might even argue that one of the most important skills in critical thinking itself is a taking hold of one's emotions and then rationally considering the presented information.

When teaching critical-thinking courses, I sometimes demonstrate the power of how emotions can bias our behavior by telling the students that I am going to bring out my son's pet tarantula, named Harry. I then proceed to tell them that, when he walks out of the jar onto the first person's hand, they must very carefully transfer the spider by letting it walk to the next person's hand, and so on and so forth. I also tell them that my son is very fond of his pet spider, and I do not wish any damage to come to him. So the students must be very careful in allowing the spider to walk from one of their hands to the next. As I'm saying this, I start to observe any students who might be squirming in their seats. This indicates to me that they might be arachnophobes – that is to say that they have a great fear (or phobia) of spiders. I then tell them that there is, in fact, no spider but that, in less than a second, their brain had started sending the rest of their body messages to basically flee or to fight. They experienced an increase in adrenaline from specific neuro-endocrine influences, which began a process whereby their bodies started to convert sugars to energy. There would also have been an increase in heart and breathing rates. This preparatory time to get ready to respond to the perceived threat all occurs in under a second. This is just one way in which our own bodies bias our behavior. You could be the bravest person on the planet, but when presented with a trigger of a phobia, you would be rendered quite helpless.

Discussing issues that we find emotionally-charged often creates an environment in which controlling our biases becomes extremely difficult. If you are passionate about a particular topic – say, in favor of medical assistance with death – it may become very difficult to consider what the other side has to say, especially if you have had a personal experience with a particular issue. We will return to this issue in the final chapter of the book. But it is very important for us to look into a mirror and consider why we are so passionate about a particular issue. We usually have heated discussions with our friends, relatives, work mates, colleagues, etc., so we better figure out how it is we wish to get along. Understanding how our biases influence our thoughts and our actions is one of the clearest ways to help us better understand *why* we have disagreements.

Take a moment and think about a particular issue on which you have very strong views. It can be about politics, sex, religion, sports, medicine, or Dancing with the Stars. Think about the processes that have led you to become so convinced of your view, and why you might be less willing or even *un*willing to consider what the other side has to say. This type of bias plays out quite clearly at sporting events. When fans cheer for their team, and a player from the other side makes a fantastic play, it is often very difficult for the opposing team's fans to acknowledge this feat. I cannot tell you the number of times I've watched mild-mannered friends abandon reason, fairness, and sportsmanship in an effort to win at a particular recreational sport. And then there are the soccer moms and dads who become over-the-top fanatics when watching their kids play. The very values of athletics, such as fun, sportsmanship, and teamwork, are often eclipsed by the desire to win a competition.

(v) Age, Health, and Sex

I must confess that in my advanced years of middle-age, I tend to understand, discuss, believe, and act differently in some ways now than I did as a younger man and certainly as a boy. So age definitely does influence and bias how we perceive and understand information and act upon it. This is simply a brute fact of life. The passage from innocence to experience is inevitable. I do not feel differently than I did when I was in my 20s. But I have experienced more at my current age, and so have a greater capacity to understand and consider and deliberate on issues than I did as a younger man. That's not to say that it's any better or any worse, but age is a factor that biases our understanding of information. For example, when I was 8 years old, my older brother Brad brought home an album from the record store and played it for the very first time. It was *Led Zeppelin II*. When he played a song called "Whole Lotta Love", and Robert Plant sang the words "I'm gonna give you every inch of my love…" I thought it meant that he must love someone very much. Like when a child is asked how much he loves his mother and he holds his arms open wide and says: "This much, Mommy!" As I grew older, my knowledge of sexual education increased, and so did my understanding of what Mr. Plant actually meant by those lyrics.

The same could be said for health. As our health changes, our views about issues can be affected or biased because of suffering, pain, or general poor health. Considering important issues just doesn't seem to have the same effect on us when we are busy fighting pain or discomfort due to ill health. And this is entirely understandable. Since there is nothing more important than our health, it follows that when we are not feeling well, little else matters. And so we must be aware of how our health status and the health status of others will bias the manner in which they interpret, consider, and act on information. And just in case you're wondering, the reason some elderly people are cranky is because they're often in constant pain or discomfort. It's sometimes tough to give a damn when you feel like crap.

As for the differences of sex, much of the literature on sexuality defines us humans on a spectrum from male to female. For the most part, the majority of our species are definitively male or female. But there are trans-gendered people who defy such strict categorization. And unfortunately, they can face serious identity problems and social backlash due to ignorance and misunderstanding. And so I want to be clear and state that I am concentrating my treatment of sexual biases predominantly on either ends of the spectrum of male or female. And please keep in mind that this has nothing to do with social or civil rights. Both sexes and the transgendered all have exactly the same rights. What I am referring to instead is the idea that the different biological makeup of males and females has led to distinctions in behaviors that can bias the manner in which information is considered and acted upon.

Humans are biologically dimorphic. That means males tend to be taller, larger, and stronger, with more muscle mass. Females have more estrogen hormone while males have more testosterone. Males tend to be more violent and aggressive. If you really need proof of this, we simply need to look at the world statistics for aggression, crime, murder, and criminal behavior. Men outrank women in this regard by over 9 to 1. But aside from these biological differences, there have been numerous studies into the physiological, hormonal, and neuronal differences between males and females, which have provided important information in the treatment of gender-specific diseases, the function of medications, different procedures for surgeries, etc. Although genetically, males and females differ only by a single Y chromosome, both sexes differ considerably in so many ways that we must realize that these differences will bias the way in which both sexes interpret, revise, retain, and act upon information.

Cultural Biases

As we have seen above, several biological factors have considerable influence over what we believe and how we act. Culture, however, is just as important because there are hundreds of developed cultures throughout the world. It should come as little surprise that social norms and cultural biases will influence the way we see, understand, and interact in the world. Here are just a few of the main types of cultural biases.

(i) Family Upbringing

How were you raised and by whom? Did you come from a home with a mother and father? A single-parent home? One with two dads or two moms? Were you raised by your siblings, relatives, or grandparents? Or were you raised by squirrels in the wilds of Canada? Our family life greatly influences how we see and understand the world. How strict or lax your care-givers or parents were in regards to your behavior will have a profound impact on you. Some of us were given a curfew to be home at a given time. Others were not. Was it a family rule that you had to eat everything on your plate before leaving the table? Did you have to do chores around the house? Were you allowed to date any person you liked? If you are gay, how was this dealt with in the home?

Families develop entire lifestyles and habits around how things get done in a day. Who takes out the trash, or does the dishes, or cuts the lawn, or looks after the shopping, and what television programs and Internet sites are suitable for viewing, and so on … these are all aspects of home life that influence or bias your behavior later in life. Violating such rules of the family household can and often does lead to challenges. Consider your behavior right now and think for a moment on how much of your day-to-day life is regulated by family patterns of behavior developed from the time you were born.

(ii) Ethnicity

The topic of immigration seems to be a constant concern in the U.S. and elsewhere throughout the world. People within one country become angry over the number of so-called "foreigners" invading and taking jobs away from its citizens. This type of hatred – or xenophobia – is a complex issue, but it often centers on differences in ethnicity. How we have come to define ourselves ethnically often plays a crucial role in how we understand issues. The values, customs, habits, and rituals of our various ethnicities can present barriers of understanding and incite dislike for others simply because they do not belong to the same group. For the most part, we tolerate and even celebrate the ethnic differences we find in our multicultural communities. But we still find that the beliefs, rituals, and actions of one ethnic group often clash with those of another. We have seen this type of ethnic hatred carried out in much more horrific forms today with warring in Syria, the Congo, Darfur, India/Pakistan, etc. Before you can become a better thinker, you need to consider to what extent your ethnic values and attachment to ethnic ways of life influences the ways in which you see the world and consider any issue.

(iii) Religion

It will come as little surprise that religion has had a considerable influence on human behavior for thousands of years and still does so today. If you happen to be religious, ask yourself how you came to develop your current metaphysical beliefs. The most common path of religious indoctrination comes to us from our parents. But there are many cases in which, as adults, we choose a particular religion for specific reasons. One of the greatest appeals to religious practice is the communal sense of support that can be found when like-minded individuals gather for a common purpose. There is no lack of evidence indicating the neural rewards that come not only with religious conviction but in celebrating that conviction within a community. And there is little doubt that religiously-motivated people have done wonderful and amazing things for humanity.

Religious belief provides people with outlooks on life that greatly influence how they think and act – both positively and negatively. But there are times when dissonance and disagreement arises due to conflicts between faith and science. For example, many devout or orthodox world religions do not accept homosexuality as a fact of biology but instead see it as a life choice that violates their god's wishes. To be a homosexual, then, is to act in ways that are in direct opposition to how a particular god wants us to behave. So if a devout person of faith happens to have a close relation – such as a son or a daughter – who happens to be gay, it may be difficult to reconcile their love of their child with the will of their god. And this is not an easy reconciliation. In fact, many students have told me that their parents have stopped speaking to them after they have come out as gay, due to their family's religious beliefs. I am not deliberately attempting to bash religious belief here, but simply trying to demonstrate how powerful this bias can be when considering information. We will return to this topic in the final chapter of the book.

(iv) Geographic Location

Ask yourself now in which part of the world you were raised. If you have always lived in a developed part of the world, how do you think your views on the world, yourself, and others might differ if you were raised in a developing nation thousands of miles from where you now live? The very fact that you live in a particular part of the world will have a profound influence on how you interpret and act on information. How someone in the U.K. will understand the Syrian conflict will be different from those who live within Middle-Eastern countries. But geographic location can be even more specific than this. For example, consider the identities and differences between provinces in Canada, states in the U.S., regions of England, India, Australia, Mexico, etc. Rivalries often develop between neighboring cities, like the fictional rivalry between Springfield and Shelbyville in *The Simpsons*.

The sense of regional community that can develop in a given part of the world can become thoroughly ingrained in our lives. This instills within us a comparative ability to view differing customs, actions, and attitudes in a way that might make us think, "That's not how we do things around here." So even our regional geography can bias us according to our preferred in-group ways of doing things.

(v) Education

The concept of education can be defined in a very broad sense, ranging from information taught at home to more formal settings, such as primary, middle, secondary, and post-secondary institutions. Just think about how differently students are taught in urban classrooms in the U.S. compared to that of an all-boys Taliban school in rural Pakistan. In the U.S., all children have access to school systems, which generally teach boys and girls equally. The Taliban, however, teaches boys only, and the main learning text is the Koran. For mathematics skills, boys have been asked to count with AK-47s, and to subtract by killing off members of rival groups. So where and how you were educated will contribute greatly to how you interpret, revise, retain, and act on information.

One of the central purposes of education is to open the minds of those seeking knowledge, and to impart upon them important, interesting, and helpful information along with sound critical-thinking skills. But education can also be used to indoctrinate specific beliefs, thereby stifling free and critical thinking, along with introspection and the thirst for knowledge. Take a moment to think a about how you were educated and the ways in which this has influenced you in your abilities to think critically.

(vi) Friends

The influence our friends have on us is undeniable. From the time of our youth, we have been actively involved in making friends and becoming associated with an intricate connection of influences. Take a moment to think back about that most awkward developmental stage in life: adolescence. With our brains awash in a bath of hormonal soup and our bodies adjusting to bigger and different parts, we began to see ourselves independently from parental guidance and control. Peer and group pressure have contributed to how we view ideas and issues, and sometimes conformity is much easier than independence. Since it is virtually impossible for any of us to live in total isolation, unaffected by others, the friendships we make have lasting impressions on us. Something to keep in mind at this point is how influential *you* are on your network of friends and how influential *they* are on you. To what degree do you or can you have meaningful discussions with your friends? Do you always tend to agree? We saw earlier how easy it is to agree. How do you and your friends deal with disagreement? Can you accept that you will have differences of opinions?

There is a classic example that demonstrates how easy it is for people to conform. In a prank show from the 1960s and 70s, called *Candid Camera*, three people get onto an elevator in which there is a single gentleman in a trench coat holding the doors open for them. When all three people get on the elevator, they face the wall of the elevator rather than the doors. In a short while, the man in the trench coat joins them and turns around and faces the wall. There have been other psychological experiments demonstrating conformity to group opinion and behavior. During the 1950s, Professor

Solomon Asch conducted a series of conformity experiments at Swarthmore College, which continues to influence conformity experiments today. In one of his experiments, a group of men look at three lines on a piece of paper, all of which have different lengths. They are then asked to determine if a separate line matches the lengths of either of the other three. All the males are secretly a part of the study with only one male unknowingly being the test subject. The first two or three examples are easy to determine and all agree which line is the match. However, on the fourth try, the line clearly is shorter than the one to which all men agree. In the majority of the trials, the test subject ends up agreeing with the rest of the men even though he knows it is clearly wrong.

One of the most striking contemporary experiments demonstrating conformity involves a group of actors and one subject sitting in a room in which a fire is staged. Smoke begins to pour into the room from beneath a doorway and a smoke alarm goes off; yet none of the people leave the room. The one test subject often appears nervous and agitated, but more times than not, does not leave the room or investigate the source of the fire. Even when there is perceived threat to a person's health, this can be overridden by peer pressure and group conformity. Such experiments make obvious the need for us to be aware of the extent to which such external influences can bias our thinking and our behavior.

(vii) Media

We are constantly inundated with information coming from various forms of media, such as the Internet, television, movies, music, newspapers, magazines, art, etc. But as we saw in the Introduction, there has been an increasing rise in what is known as "fake news" (especially online). This involves information that can appear on Twitter or Facebook or other such sites, in which people have deliberately created fake or false information to appear as though it is reliable. As we saw in Step One, *reliability* is one of the universal foundational criteria upon which our premises must rest. So we must be on our guard against such fake accounts of information. We must learn to become media literate. We have to empower ourselves with the critical-thinking skills that will allow us to recognize when information is not factual. So we cannot simply believe everything we see or read just because it's on the Internet, or in a magazine, or on television.

You must ask yourself where you get your information. Do you get it mostly from online sources? Television? Newspapers? Magazines? The schoolyard? Your neighbor? Be aware that all information – no matter which type – comes to you already biased (including this very book). There is no such thing as bias-neutral information. Whether or not you watch *Fox and Friends* or *The Daily Show,* turn on CNN News, MSNBC or Al Jazeera, the information you receive will have a particular political slant to it. And recognizing the political ideologies behind the media you receive will empower you with the ability to acknowledge how a particular source wants you to interpret the information. Never forget that everyone has an agenda – from your local librarian to Donald Trump. And it is very difficult for humans to play fairly and get along, especially when it comes to discussing important issues. And this is because our agendas and our biases often get in the way and limits us in this regard.

(viii) Bias Check: Biases are Filters of Information

If you haven't already, you now need to understand that everything you think and everything you do is the result of your biological and cultural biases. You now need to do a *Bias Check* and become aware that any new information presented to you must pass through a series of biased filters before you can accept it, reject it, or remain neutral to it.

Bias Filters

We often favor information that confirms our own biases. This is normal. And this is what it means in many respects to be human. However, in critical thinking, we develop the ability to acknowledge what our biases are in an effort to more fairly understand why it is we believe what we do and why it is that we act according to those particular beliefs. In this way, we become more critically reflective of our beliefs and ideas and opinions. And in this way, we can become more humble in our assertions and fairer in our treatment of others whose opinions, ideas, and beliefs may differ from our own. As with news services, it is often difficult to diminish our own biases and vested interests in order to objectively consider and act upon the *facts*. So we must learn to recognize social biases, both in others and in ourselves, because these often distort sound reasoning, which leads to unwarranted conclusions. It is extremely difficult to acknowledge our own biases, especially when we are emotionally connected to a particular issue. But in order to argue clearly and present our ideas in a precise, consistent, and fair manner, we must learn to recognize and compensate for our biases. And this is not easy. That is why critical thinking takes time, and effort, and repetition. And it is why the most difficult part of becoming a good critical thinker is to acknowledge any biases in yourself that may distort your reasoning.

Bias Check

Take some time to do a Bias Check and consider what biases have influenced you the most at this particular time in your life, when you think about important issues like abortion, euthanasia, gun control, religion, sex, etc. Take a moment to write down what you perceive to be your most influential biases.

Biological Biases:

1. Genetic:

2. Neuropsychological:

3. Emotional:

4. Age, Sex, and Health:

Social Biases:

1. Ethnicity:

2. Family:

3. Religion:

4. Geography:

5. Education:

6. Friends:

7. Media:

Once you have made a list of your biases, you will be in a better position to understand why it is you believe what you do and act the way you do. In so doing, you will be better equipped to recognize biases in others.

Confirmation Bias, Fairness, and Getting Along

And now we come to the most difficult part of the book: Acknowledging our biases, playing fairly, and getting along.

Everyone likes to be right – or at least the *feeling* of being right. This feeling of being right provides us with a neuro-chemical reward, accompanied by a sense of control, empowerment, security, and status. As we grow and mature, so too do our beliefs become entrenched through various biological and cultural biases. It is perfectly normal then that we are all victims of what is called "confirmation bias". Take a moment to consider your current beliefs regarding, say, gun control (another topic we shall consider in the final chapter). Why do you believe what you now do in relation to this topic? In what context did you develop your views? What evidence do you rely upon to support your views? Whether you believe all guns should be destroyed or everyone should be able to carry loaded weapons anywhere they travel, your entrenched views developed over time. And whether you are aware of this or not, we tend to look more favorably toward information and evidence that supports our views and ignore that which disconfirms or fails to support our views. This type of positive-feedback looping of support feeds and confirms our already-established biases about issues. Perhaps a definition of confirmation bias is best summed up in a paraphrase of Paul Simon's lyrics from the song 'The Boxer': A person hears what they want to hear and disregards the rest. We can never escape our biases. But at least we can acknowledge them and do our best to make sure that they have not clouded our abilities to think critically about important issues.

The ancient Egyptians and Greeks had a wonderful model for humankind's struggle with such influences. They used the analogy of a chariot rider. I wish to borrow and modify this allegory to visually demonstrate the difficulty we face when practicing critical thinking. If we can imagine the charioteer being represented as our reason, then the horses can be represented as both the facts and our biases. On the one hand, the facts lead us on a fairly straight path of evidence. However, our biases influence the manner in which we perceive and frame the facts according to our current habits of thinking. As critical thinkers, we must try to control our biases so that we can steer them to better follow where the facts will lead us down the path of evidence towards the truth.

As we saw earlier, fairness acts as the *Golden Rule of Dialogue*. In other words, we must abide by the rules of fairness when considering the ideas and biases of others, just as we would want others to do for us. Playing fairly and getting along are some of the first rules instilled in kids when they are sent off to play with other children. And yet they are rules we all too soon abandon as we age. And the reason is that much that happens in the world is perceived by many to be unfair. There is precious little justice in life. And we are often victims of unfairness – sometimes to the point of cruelty, despair, and ruin. So for me to say that we must "play fairly" may sound like a piece of advice you would just as soon skip over. But I must tell you, as an ideal, fairness always wins out over deception and cheating. As I mentioned earlier, fairness is the *Cornerstone of Critical Thinking*. If everyone plays by the rules of critical thinking and abides by the *Golden Rule of Dialogue*, everyone will get more of what they want. But this requires cooperation and understanding.

And let's face it, sometimes, it's not easy to be fair. We all like to win. We all have egos, goals for status and resources, ambitions, biases, and the drive to succeed (some more than others). So it should come as no surprise that we like to be right when it comes to making a point or taking a position. When confronted with an opposing view, one of the most difficult things to do in critical thinking is to accept it as a good argument (even if you disagree with it). To use a sports analogy, this is not unlike acknowledging a great goal scored against your team. Good educators should be able to read student assignments without having their personal, political, or philosophical biases affect the grade. Likewise, good bosses should acknowledge when an employee makes a good point counter to his/her own. As well, good politicians should admit to their biases (and mistakes) and acknowledge good ideas from opposing party members. We are not all going to agree all of the time. Disagreements are a fact of life. But by understanding how our biases and the biases of others influence the ways in which we interpret, understand, and act on information, we can better appreciate why differences of opinion exist, and why disagreements develop. In so doing, we can go a long way towards understanding the uniqueness of individual thought. This will allow us to more amicably and fairly resolve differences, mediate disagreements, and initiate dialogue that is productive and respectful to both sides, regardless of the outcome.

B is for Bias. Now that we know what arguments are and how biases contribute to the ways in which we interpret, understand, revise, and act upon information, we can turn our attention towards the third step to better thinking: *context*. As we shall see, understanding the context in which information arises is just as important as the information itself.

Step 3: C is for Context

To take the next step, we need to consider context, which is actually the time, the place, and the circumstances in which information is considered. In other words, context is all about the "back story". This includes things like the setting in which the information takes place, the time in which it occurred, and certainly the circumstances in which that information is found. These factors, along with other factual forms of background information, allow us to more fairly assess information. And we want to be fair in our assessment of information. Otherwise, we can misinterpret information and mistakenly analyze it according to our misinterpretation, which is not fair to the intention of the person who stated it.

There are many examples of such contextual misinterpretations throughout history, where people misinterpreted information and took that information entirely out of context. During the summer of 1984, I can recall one of the most famous examples being Bruce Springsteen's hit song "Born in the USA". This is a very catchy tune, which has what is known in the record industry as a "great hook". A hook is often a catchy, lyrical phrase. In Springsteen's song, the hook is found in the lines that continuously repeat the phrase: "(I was) born in the USA". Possibly because of the catchiness of the hook, it has become one of the most misinterpreted songs in the history of rock 'n roll. You may know others, but this one stands out as particularly relevant as an example of how important context can be.

So what is the song is actually about? It's really a social commentary by Springsteen on the misuse of the rights of American soldiers during the Vietnam War:

Got in a little hometown jam
So they put a rifle in my hand
Sent me off to a foreign land
To go and kill the yellow man[7]

Springsteen is commenting that young American men were sent to faraway places to kill foreign people for political reasons beyond their control. And then when they came back to America, they did not have the support required for them to continue on with their lives:

Come back home to the refinery
Hiring man said, "Son, if it was up to me"
Went down to see my V.A. man
He said, "Son, don't you understand"[8]

It's a telling commentary about a specific dark point of time in American history during the 1960s and early '70s. However, because the hook in the chorus is just so darn catchy, it became widely misinterpreted as being very pro-American. Chanted at halftime at many a sporting event, the chorus – "I was born in the USA" – continues to evoke feelings of pride in millions of Americans. The main problem, though, is contextual. Their feelings of patriotism are generated on a misinterpretation of the song's intended meaning. It's not as though we don't validate emotional responses. That would be missing the point. What we want to point out, though, is that the patriotism felt in the chorus of the song's lyrics are quite misguided, and therefore entirely *irrelevant* to the interpretation of the song. Ronald Reagan was among the first to misinterpret and try to use Mr. Springsteen's song during his presidential

---

[7]   Springsteen, Bruce. "Born in the USA." Columbia Records, June 4, 1984. Recorded the E Street Band. Produced by Chuck Plotkin and Jon Landau at The Power Station and The Hit Factory in New York City.

[8]   Ibid.

candidacy in 1984. Because of its patriotic tone, the song represented a premise (or wall) in support of Reagan's conclusion (or roof) that he should be President of the United States. Unfortunately, because it was taken out of context, it failed to satisfy the universal foundational criterion of relevance. Not only did Reagan's campaign party misinterpret the context of the song, Springsteen's legal representatives notified Reagan's publicist that he did not have permission to do so, and they subsequently stopped using the song as a propaganda anthem for his candidacy for presidency. For the record, Reagan ended up winning the '84 election over Walter Mondale with 49 states.

When we consider information, regardless of what media is its source – newspaper, Internet, television, etc. – we must be cautious and ensure that the information has been presented with enough background information that we are able to appreciate the context more fully, so we can provide a fairer assessment of that information. Otherwise, if we react too quickly, and form opinions, whatever we say as a critique of that information could end up being entirely *irrelevant*. To commit such an error, as you will see in greater detail in step six, is known as the "Strawman Fallacy". Basically, a person commits this fallacy when they misinterpret information, and then proceed to criticize it based on their own misinterpretation. This renders everything they say as *irrelevant*. And this is because they have not fairly understood the intended context in which the information was presented. So the falsely interpreted argument that they are attacking is made out of straw – not a real argument.

How then, are we to consider information that comes to us regarding actions that are taking place thousands of miles from us? For example, how much context can we confirm regarding information we receive about what is occurring in Syria, Somalia, Saskatchewan, etc.? My privileged view of trying to understand what is happening in other parts of the world has limited contextual background. Since I am removed from their world, and I experience it through the filtered and biased views of various news editors (as well as through the filters of my own biases), I may not be getting the complete story and may find myself divorced from some of the contextual nature of the activities that are taking place.

So then, to what extent can we trust the information we receive through various forms of media? We just saw how important satisfying the universal foundational criterion of relevance is in understanding context. We must also be on our guard to make sure we abide by the foundational criterion of *reliability* in our efforts to appreciate the context of information. If the information presented to us has not been established in a reliable manner, we may not be able to appropriately comment on the actual intent or factual nature of the information. As we saw during the 2016 U.S. presidential election race, there was a great deal of fake news circulating online, not only from Facebook and Twitter but from dozens of other sites as well. If we use any of the information from such fake sources as premises for our conclusions, we have failed to appreciate the context in which that information was presented, and therefore, have failed to satisfy the universal criterion of reliability. In this manner, we would not be treating the information or those to whom the information applies fairly, because such information has come from unreliable (i.e. fake news) sources. And remember, we can't just believe anything we want to simply because it *feels* true. Truth and facts are not subject to feelings. The world does not care if you *feel* that Bigfoot exists. The facts of the matter state otherwise. Show me some facts though, such as a body of a sasquatch – either living or dead – and I must follow the facts to where the evidence leads.

Not only must we consider how *reliable* our sources of information are regarding context, we are also led to consider the universal criterion of *sufficiency*: When is enough background information, time, and circumstance, *sufficient* to provide the context required for us to make a fair interpretation of information? There is no hard and fast rule about this. However, we must be diligent in assuring that we have determined as much contextual background material as possible, to make an informed decision regarding the information. In this way, when context is sufficient, we can more fairly interpret what is being presented, and why the information is being presented in the way it is. One activity that I often practice in class, to fairly establish context, is to have students re-state another's argument back to them. Once there is agreement that the intention of the information was fairly interpreted, and the context has been sufficiently determined, commentary and dialogue about the content of the argument can proceed more fairly.

How many times have you said or heard the following phrase: "That was taken out of context." This basically refers to an unfair interpretation of an issue due either to a lack of factual information or a misunderstanding of the surroundings or circumstances in which the information was situated. Now we also need to realize that even though we will take the necessary steps to assure the reliability of the sources of the information, and that the information is sufficient to warrant fair interpretation and response to the information, this is never a closed matter. In other words, we should always be open to the possibility of changing our minds and our opinions. To refuse to do so would be dogmatic to the point of blind ignorance. In other words, we must constantly entertain the possibility that our beliefs could be wrong. This is simply fair. There may still be further information to be revealed that gives us reason to revise our current understanding of the situation. For this reason, we must always be ready to adjust our views based on new or unknown information or evidence. We must be open-minded, but not so much so that our brains fall out. For example, I will believe that Bigfoot exists whenever the appropriate reliable evidence is sufficiently presented. Otherwise, I currently have no reason to believe in such a being. But I am not entirely doubtful that the possibility exists for me to change my mind should future evidence warrant this.

A Cautionary Device for Considering Context

In order to be cautious in our consideration of the context of information, we might wish to hedge our bets, as it were, by stating a conditional or *proviso* on the information itself. In other words, forming arguments is dependent upon the condition that one *believes* to be in possession of enough relevant, reliable, and sufficient information to faithfully capture the context in which that information is found. The condition can be stated in various forms:

1. "Based on the information I have before me, and the context in which it is placed, I believe . . ."

2. "All things considered, I now believe . . ."

3. "Given what I now know, I believe . . ."

So the proper understanding of context is very much about playing fairly. You want to be sure that you have interpreted the information in the best spirit of its intention. This is in keeping with the *Golden Rule of Dialogue*. In essence, it is what you would expect others to do with *your* claims. So you shall do the same for them. As we touched on earlier, you may be wondering why we should play fairly. The rest of the world doesn't, so wouldn't doing so just make us chumps? Or suckers? I don't believe so. Because playing fairly and cooperating is the main way in which all of us can keep some semblance of order and respect in a world where there are so many cheaters. Cooperation will always win out over individuality and selfishness. In this way, whenever we play fairly, we all get more of what we want. It is often the case that, when people feel as though they're not being treated fairly, it leads to hostility, anger, and resentment, and makes the process of understanding, mediation, and resolution so much more difficult. Getting along is often the direct result of playing fairly and abiding by agreed-upon rules. We don't like it when a sports team cheats or "bends the rules" in order to win (I'm looking at you, New England Patriots). This is something innately within us of which we disapprove. It is no surprise then that we should feel the same way when having heated or intense discussions. But fairness is and will always be the

Six Steps to Better Thinking

Cornerstone of Critical Thinking. The sooner we realize this, the quicker we will be able to get along and the better it will be for all of us.

Here are some of the central rules for fair play and critical thinking:

1. Acknowledge your existing biases and determine how they filter the way in which you see and act in the world.

2. Make every effort to attain enough facts before formulating a position on a particular issue.

3. Make every effort to acknowledge the context in which the facts occur before formulating a position on a particular issue. Use a conditional like: "All things considered, this is what I now believe."

4. Acknowledge that, due to the way in which so many people are biased differently, there are going to be disagreements on many issues.

5. Be open to the possibility of revising your position.

Just as we see in the ancient Indian parable of the blind men who all believe an elephant to be different things, we must appreciate the importance of bias and context when it comes to interpreting, understanding, and acting upon information. We need to be careful when interpreting information to make sure that we have established enough background information to be able to acknowledge the context in which the information is being presented. By understanding how our biases affect our judgments – and considering the amount of information we have attained, along with the context in which it is presented – we can go a long way toward increasing the likelihood of a fair account, which will ultimately lead to more effective communication for all parties.

We have now mentally walked up the first three steps to better thinking. These literally involved the basics or ABC's of critical thinking. We will now consider three more steps which focus on the more technical aspects of critical thinking and will start with the very important skill of diagramming arguments.

Step 4: D is for Diagram

To diagram an argument is the most technical – and perhaps most boring – of the critical thinking tools within the skill set. But it is arguably one of the most important. Diagramming arguments allows us to literally draw what the structure of an argument looks like: not only our own arguments, but those of others as well. This skill allows us to see what peoples' argumentative "houses" look like. This puts us in a better position to consider the strength or weaknesses of their premises. Diagramming an argument also extends upon the value of fairness within critical thinking, because it allows us to be able to express our interpretation of another person's argument in the best possible light, in order to most accurately and fairly depict the intention of their argument. Once we are able to identify the structure of a person's argument from their overall conclusion (roof) to their supporting premises (walls), we are in a better position to understand the manner in which they have satisfied, or failed to satisfy, the foundational universal criteria of consistency, simplicity, relevance, reliability, and sufficiency. So it is a skill that literally allows us to *see* another person's argument or our own. Diagramming also allows us to focus particularly on the key components of a person's argument. It does this by weeding out the most important premises from what can be called "noise". Noise may provide setting or context: "It was the best of times, it was the worst of times…"but may not be directly relevant to the overall argument itself. Diagramming simply allows us to be better prepared in distinguishing between the premises and the conclusion.

You are confronted with arguments every day of your life. If you spend any amount of time online, you will be inundated with an enormous number of advertisements. If you watch television, they're everywhere. Even if you go to the movies, you will find advertisements. Whenever you see members of congress or parliament engaged in discussion, they are stating arguments for why they believe their ideas should be the ones to be adopted by society. Whenever you have discussions with family, friends, workmates, or complete strangers, you will find that you are presenting and exchanging ideas in the form of arguments. Even if you just talk about the weather, you may be stating conclusions regarding how much you enjoy or dislike it and then subsequently stating why.

So when you come across an argument, you must first determine what the conclusion is. After that, what follows will be the premises and perhaps some noise as well. To determine the conclusion, you must ask yourself what you believe the person's overall point is that they're trying to make. With advertisements, the conclusion is always (or usually) hidden: "You should buy this product." Once we can determine what that conclusion is, we can then go about determining what the supporting premises are, and whether or not we believe they have satisfied the foundational criteria of consistency, simplicity, relevance, reliability, and sufficiency.

Before we continue, we need to take a minute to become familiar with some abbreviations that stand for the various parts of an argument.

All premises are abbreviated as a capital "**P**" and are numbered, P1, P2, P3 etc., depending on how many premises are offered.

The conclusion is abbreviated as a capital "**C**".

Arrows are then used to show the connection between the premises and the conclusion. For example, consider this argument:

> I think you are a great person. You are kind to strangers. You give your time and money to charities. And you are always willing to help a person in need.

In this example, three premises support the conclusion. To diagram this argument, you would draw the following:

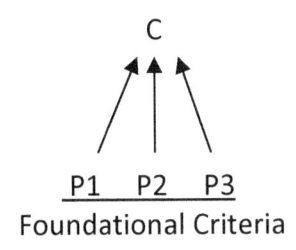

```
         C
        ↑↑↑
        /|\
       / | \
      P1 P2 P3
```
Foundational Criteria

So the three basic premises (P1, P2, and P3) are the supports for the conclusion (C), just as walls support a roof. The conclusion in this example is the statement that someone is a great person, *because* they are kind, giving, and helpful to others. Since this argument is not extremely complex, it is called a "Simple Argument". There is also no noise to separate from the premises or conclusion. In terms of considering the foundational criteria, all three premises appear to be internally consistent. That is, such qualities tend to define a person as "good". However, we have no idea who the person is and so cannot determine the external consistency of the premises. For example, there are plenty of people who could be kind to strangers, provide money and time to charities, and help people in need, and yet they are quite cruel to animals or their own family members. The premises appear to satisfy the criterion of simplicity, and they all appear to be relevant in support of the conclusion. And we are currently unable to determine either the reliability or sufficiency of the premises, because we simply have no idea to whom, specifically, the person is referring.

There is a second type of premises, which are called "main premises" and are appropriately abbreviated as "**MP**". As we saw above, a premise (P) is a support for a conclusion (C), but it can also support a main premise (MP). Consider the following example stated by Marjory Fox:

John Doyle is experienced, courageous, and honest. These are all the types of qualities that make a good senator. That's why I think you should vote for John Doyle.

In this argument, the conclusion (or roof) is that people should vote for John Doyle to become a senator. But unlike the first example, this argument contains a main premise as well. Can you spot it? It's the claim that his experience, courage, and honesty are the types of qualities that makes a good senator. If we were to diagram this argument, it would look something like this:

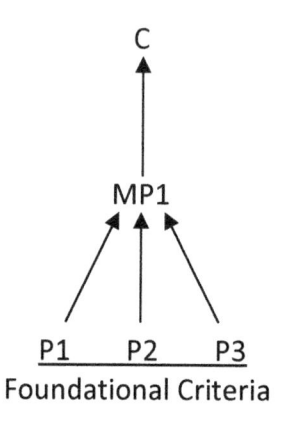

```
           C
           ↑
           |
          MP1
         ↑ ↑ ↑
        /  |  \
       P1  P2  P3
     Foundational Criteria
```

As we can see from the above example, conclusions are abbreviated as a capital "C". But just as there are two types of premises – P and MP – there are two types of conclusions as well, abbreviated as "**C**" and "**HC**". The conclusion can either be stated (C) or hidden (HC). As with the example above, when a conclusion is stated, it becomes labeled as "C". But when it is unstated, we need to label it as "HC". And as we have seen, the most common arguments to have hidden conclusions are advertisements. As we noted, above, the conclusion to the majority of advertisements is generally the same: "*Buy this product.*" But this is rarely actually stated in the ad. Instead, advertisers use other techniques to try to convince you to buy their product. And if they convince you – for whatever reasons – you may buy their product and they can make money.

Now that we have visually seen how the structure of arguments can be drawn, we need to consider how we can easily spot premises and conclusions. In all arguments – whether written or verbal – we are given clues as to where these are. And so, we must search for what are called "indicator words". As their name suggests, they *indicate* to us where, precisely, the premises and conclusions can be found. Here is a partial list of both types:

Conclusion-Indicators

therefore	we may infer that
hence	I conclude that
thus	which shows/reveals that
so	*which means that*
ergo	*establishes*
then	implies
consequently	proves that
as a result	justifies
follows	supports

Premise-Indicators

since	the reason(s) is (are)
as indicated by	*for*
if	*as*
because	given that

Those indicator words that appear in italics are the most commonly used in everyday language. It should be noted that not all types of arguments will contain these terms, because they can be used in ways that indicate neither premises nor conclusions. Fortunately though, it is often the case that they *do* indicate the specific parts of an argument. And learning this distinction will take time and practice.

Christopher DiCarlo

<u>Formal Guidelines for Diagramming a Written Argument</u>

To diagram a written argument, begin by finding the conclusion. Then underline it. If you don't know what the overall point is, it may be hidden. But if you can locate it, underline it. What remains will be the premises and noise. Next, circle any words that indicate where the conclusion is and where the premises are. At this point, simply place brackets around what you believe to be individual premises. Then determine if they are basic premises (P) or a main premise (MP) and number them accordingly: P1, P2, MP1, etc.

In the Marjory Fox example, above, she maintained that:

> ^{P1}[John Doyle is experienced], ^{P2}[courageous], and ^{P3}[honest]. ^{MP1}[These are all the types of qualities which makes a good senator]. That's why I think <u>you should vote for John Doyle</u>.

The next step involves the construction of a legend. You must write out each of the Premises, Main Premises, and Conclusion. For example, in the argument above, the components of Marjory's argument would be placed in a legend in the following manner:

P1 = John Doyle is experienced
P2 = He is courageous
P3 = He is Honest
MP1 = These are all the types of qualities which makes a good senator
C = You should vote for John Doyle

The purpose of the legend is to treat the speaker's argument fairly. This will allow you to faithfully and accurately represent what you believe to be the intention of the person making the argument. Sometimes, it will be necessary to apply what is called "the principle of charity" with some of the premises. In other words, if a person uses slang or jargon, you need to present what you honestly believe was their intended meaning. For example, if someone states a premise that a politician is "out of his mind", this needs to be translated to read that they are "misguided" or "not thinking straight". In the legend, we keep an eye out for phrases containing double-negatives (e.g. "ain't got no"), as well as slang, personal assaults, etc., in order to reflect the person's argument in its best possible light. By doing so, you are *playing fair,* by interpreting and representing their intention as accurately as possible, which – in keeping with the *Golden Rule of Dialogue* – is exactly what you would expect to be done with your own argument.

After we have completed a legend of the argument, we can depict its structure. And as we saw above, Marjory's argument can be diagrammed in the following way:

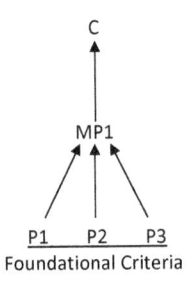

```
        C
        ↑
        |
       MP1
       ↑↑↑
       /|\
      / | \
    P1  P2  P3
  Foundational Criteria
```

So let's review. D is for Diagram. The best way to assure that you understand another person's argument is to mentally or physically draw out its structure.

Here is a basic checklist for diagramming arguments:

1. Determine the overall point or conclusion that the person is trying to make. If it is a written argument, start by underlining the conclusion (C). If the conclusion is not clearly stated, it is probably hidden (HC).

2. Consider whether or not indicator words have been used. If so, circle them.

3. Place brackets around and number the various basic or main premises.

4. Create a legend and be charitable in adjusting any wording of their premises if necessary.

5. Build a house with the conclusion on top, premises supporting, and universal criteria as the foundation.

Complex Arguments

Keep in mind that the examples above are called *simple* arguments. Most arguments we experience are much longer and far more *complex*. And this is why it is so important to be able to diagram them. It better allows us to understand them in terms of their structure. Consider this complex argument:

> We have got to close down Guantanamo Bay Detention Camp. First of all, the costs to the U.S. are staggeringly high. One report estimates as much as 5 billion dollars has been spent on this detention camp by U.S. tax dollars. At this rate, we will never recover our costs. Secondly, the information from the prisoners has not been very helpful with ending terrorism. With the use of torture strategies, the U.S. has damaged its reputation. And through the increased statements of denying that torture has been used, our citizens have lost confidence in their government. And there have been far too many 'accidental' deaths caused by so-called resistance to cooperate. And then there is the fact that the so-called "War on Terror" is largely an unwinnable war. You never know if you've won such a war, because terrorist acts continue to happen. And this is happening in other countries as well. Because the war on terror is unwinnable, we should get our troops out of there as soon as possible. The men behind bars have been treated brutally. And because of this, morale is at an all-time low. This is now the longest war in U.S. history. The news media doesn't help morale much either; they keep showing images of how often Gitmo continues to fail in its purpose. (Trinity Gibson, Lethbridge, AB).

To diagram this argument, it is going to take a little more time and patience. But we use the exact same techniques as were used in the simpler arguments. Just remember to follow the checklist. In this argument, Ms. Gibson wants to convince us that the U.S. government should shut down Guantanamo Bay Detention Camp. When we ask ourselves why she would want us to believe this, we can see a number of basic and main premises offered. The first main premise is the costs to U.S. taxpayers. She supports this with some basic premises stating how much it is costing the U.S. taxpayers and the unlikelihood of recovering the costs. Her second main premise is that the information from the prisoners has not been very helpful with ending terrorism. Her basic premises to support this include the damage caused to the international reputation of the U.S., a loss of confidence in the government, and the result of too many 'accidental' deaths. Her third main premise is that the so-called "War on Terror" is essentially an unwinnable war. This is supported by her premise that we cannot tell when a war on terror has been won, because terrorist acts continue to happen. And this is further supported by her claim that similar wars on terror are being experienced in other countries as well. This is further reason to bring the U.S. troops out of Guantanamo Bay. And finally, the last major premise states that the brutal treatment of the prisoners has morale at an all-time low. This is supported by the claims that the length of the war is another reason why morale is low. And the media is implicated in contributing to this depiction of low morale. Regardless of whether or not you happen to agree with Ms. Gibson's argument for the closing down of Guantanamo Bay Detention Camp, your concern right now lies with the structure of her argument. When we diagram her argument, it looks like this:

<u>We have got to close down Guantanamo Bay Detention Camp</u>. First of all, ^{MP1}[the costs to the U.S. are staggeringly high]. One report estimates ^{P1}[as much as 5 billion dollars has been spent on this war by U.S. tax dollars]. At this rate, ^{P2}[we will never recover our costs]. Secondly, ^{MP2}[the information from the prisoners has not been very helpful with ending terrorism]. ^{P3}[With the use of torture strategies, the U.S. has damaged its reputation]. And ^{P4}[through the increased statements of denying that torture has been used, our citizens have lost confidence in their government]. And ^{P5}[there have been far too many 'accidental' deaths caused by so-called resistance to cooperate]. And then there is the fact that ^{MP3}[the so-called 'War on Terror' is largely an unwinnable war]. ^{P6}[You never know if you've won such a war because terrorist acts continue to happen]. And ^{P7}[this is happening in other countries as well]. Because ^{P8}[the war on terror is unwinnable, we should get our troops out of there as soon as possible]. ^{P9}[The men behind bars have been treated brutally]. And because of this, ^{MP4}[morale is at an all-time low]. ^{P10}[This is now the longest war in U.S. history]. ^{P11}[The news media doesn't help morale much either; they keep showing images of how often Gitmo continues to fail in its purpose]. (Trinity Gibson, Lethbridge, AB).

Legend

C = The U.S. government should close down Guantanamo Bay Detention Camp.
MP1 = The costs to the U.S. are staggeringly high.
P1 = As much as 5 billion dollars has been spent on this war by U.S. tax dollars.
P2 = The U.S. will never recover the costs.

MP2 = The information from the prisoners has not been very helpful with ending terrorism.
P3 = With the use of torture strategies, the U.S. has damaged its reputation.
P4 = Through the increased statements of denying that torture has been used, our citizens have lost confidence in their government.
P5 = There have been far too many "accidental" deaths caused by so-called resistance to cooperate. Translation: The lives of prisoners are being lost but under mysterious circumstances.
MP3 = The so-called "War on Terror" is largely an unwinnable war.
P6 = You never know if you've won such a war, because terrorist acts continue to happen.
P7 = This is happening in other countries as well.
P8 = The war on terror is unwinnable; we should get our troops out of there as soon as possible.
P9 = The men behind bars have been treated brutally.
MP4 = Morale at Gitmo is at an all-time low.
P10 = This is now the longest war in U.S. history.
P11 = The news media doesn't help U.S. morale because they keep showing images of how often Gitmo continues to fail in its purpose.

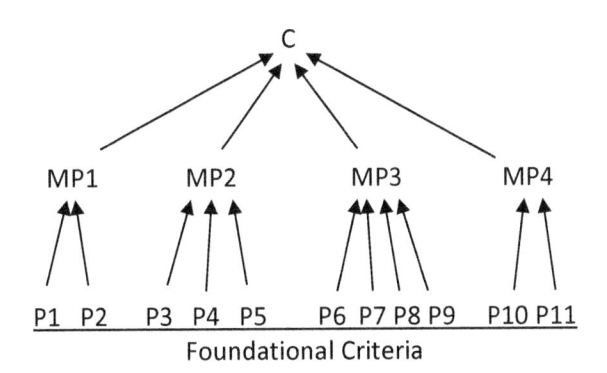

```
              C
        ↗ ↑ ↑ ↖
       /  |  \  \
      /   |   \  \
    MP1  MP2  MP3  MP4
    ↑↑   ↑↑↑  ↑↑↑↑  ↑↑
   / \   /|\  /|\\  /|\
  P1 P2 P3 P4 P5 P6 P7 P8 P9 P10 P11
  ─────────────────────────────────
           Foundational Criteria
```

As you can see, Ms. Gibson's argument is rather complex. But she has stated it in a way that is relatively easy for us to follow and understand, because there is very little noise. Many arguments are much more complex than this and would require a significant amount of time and energy to diagram. And some arguments are much simpler. For now, the best practice for diagramming is found online on blogs or in local newspaper or Internet "letters to the editor". Usually, short letters and blogs about various issues provide plenty of information in which you can practice your diagramming techniques.

> If you want to know if you are using these techniques properly, please consult the online source at:
> www.sixstepstobetterthinking.com

D is for Diagram. And all arguments can be diagrammed in this way. Some are much simpler, but many are far more complex. Every argument can be diagrammed if we take the time and exercise patience in considering its structure. Now that we have considered the ways in which it is easier for us to see the structure of an argument, it is time to move on to the next step and consider the evidence of those premises.

Step 5: E is for Evidence

There are many different types of claims that we and others make every day. Some of these claims require very little evidence in order to convince someone of our views. For example, when someone says, "It's a beautiful day today", we generally don't demand of them any supporting evidence. This is simply small talk or commentary. Other claims, however, require more evidence. And as we saw with examples of extraordinary claims, like the existence of aliens, or that the moon landing did not take place, or that Bigfoot exists, these require considerably more evidence. In determining the sufficiency of evidence, use the Sagan Principle: "Extraordinary claims require extraordinary evidence." Remember, the more spectacular or extraordinary the claim, the greater the evidence will need to be in order to support such a conclusion.

We have seen that, whenever someone makes a claim or states an argument, their premises act as supports to their conclusion. Whenever you present an argument, the burden of proof lies with you to support that claim. You must provide evidence to try to convince somebody of why you believe something to be true. As with the Sagan Principle, the stronger the claim, the greater the burden of proof, and the more convincing the evidence is going to have to be. Now, there are different types of evidence that can be supplied and various means by which to measure the effectiveness of those types of evidence.

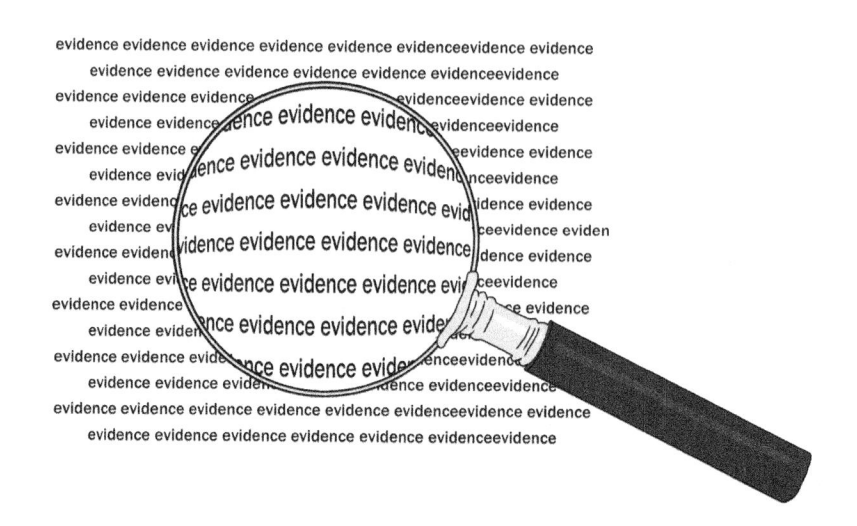

But why is evidence so important? An eighteenth-century Scottish philosopher named David Hume believed that wise people proportion themselves to the evidence. And later, a nineteenth-century British mathematician named William Kingdon Clifford summed it up well by saying, "It is wrong always, everywhere, and for anyone, to believe anything upon insufficient evidence".[9]

Evidence and Assumptions

But what counts as evidence? Consider some examples. If I told you that 1 + 1 = 2, and you said, "Prove it", what evidence could I provide, other than taking two individual things, putting them together, and telling you that I now have two of them? But if I were pressed further to justify why I believe that 1 + 1 = 2, I must ultimately confess that underlying my claim rests the *assumptions* that 1 and 2 are numbers, that the symbols + and = have meaning, and that there are rules which define the relationship between those numbers and the symbols. The same type of *assumptions* is at play

---

9 Originally published in Contemporary Review for January, 1877. Reprinted in Lectures and Essays by the late William Kindon Clifford, F.R.S., ed. Leslie Stephen and Frederick Pollock, with an Introduction by F. Pollock, 2nd Edition (London: Macmillan and Co., 1886), p.344.

when considering observations in the natural world. If I were to claim that water boils at sea level at 100°C or 212°F, assumptions are made about the properties of water, defined as molecules made up of hydrogen and oxygen, the thermal activity that takes place in heating up such a liquid, and that the state of matter of water will change from a liquid to a gas. I could then demonstrate this to you by actually boiling water, and thereby provide evidence for my claim that water boils at a specific temperature. But never forget that underlying *all* of our claims are *assumptions*. Every assertion you make assumes some underlying pre-existing information that you take to be true. Whether consciously acknowledged or not, every one of your thoughts and every one of your actions assumes some pre-existing information. The simple act of driving a car assumes that gravitational force remains constant, that the laws of force and momentum and inertia do not suddenly change, that your brakes work, and that others will continue to obey the laws of the road – all of which would make your driving much more difficult, if their consistency was not assumed.

In making any claim, the burden of proof always lies with you in supporting the claim. You must therefore provide evidence in an attempt to strengthen your argument and convince others why it is that you believe something to be true. As with the Sagan Principle, the stronger the claim, the greater the burden of proof, and the more convincing the evidence is going to have to be. Different types of evidence can be supplied depending on the context and circumstances surrounding the information. Here are four types of evidence to consider.

Anecdotal Evidence

Anecdotal evidence involves personal experience. In other words, this type of evidence is what you, as an individual, have personally experienced or encountered. We must be careful with this type of evidence, because it can lead to improper generalizations. For example, if you are the type of person who believes that women are bad drivers, then you will constantly be on the lookout for evidence that will confirm your pre-existing bias. And you will more than likely ignore evidence that runs counter to your current bias that women are bad drivers. And what started the bias in the first place might have been due to a small number of instances where examples of bad driving happened to have been done by women. And this may have led to the improper generalization, which led to the conclusion that *all* women are bad drivers. The same type of improper generalization occurs when individuals provide anecdotal evidence for witnessing the existence of aliens, or Bigfoot, or that vaccinations cause autism, or racism, misogyny, ageism, homophobia, etc. When something happens to us personally, it can leave a big impression on us. And so we naturally use those experiences as guides for our future behavior. If you have ever been food poisoned, and believe it came from a particular restaurant, you might warn others not to eat there. Or if you saw a movie recently that you didn't particularly like, you might tell people that it's not very good and that they shouldn't waste their money. But these are largely just *your* individual opinions. And we must always be on our guard against the temptation to believe that something is actually true, simply because we personally believe it to be.

Not all anecdotal evidence, however, leads to improper generalizations. There are times when it simply takes one experience to make a proper generalization. For example, the saying "once bitten, twice shy" comes into effect when we experience potentially dangerous situations. The single touching of a hot stove is often enough to teach a child to properly generalize that it might cause the same type of harm again in the future, and to be careful the next time they are near the stove.

Legal Evidence

Legal testimonials are presented in courts of law, from the municipal to the federal levels. In such cases, witnesses in a court of law swear under oath that the information they are providing is true. Sometimes eye-witness accounts are offered as evidence. At other times, so-called "expert witnesses" are brought in to support either the defense or the prosecution. But in most cases, attorneys will try to demonstrate why the opinions of the people providing testimonials for their side should be considered as valuable evidence, while testimonials from the other side should not. We need to keep in mind that the basis of legal testimony rests on the *assumption* that a person providing information or evidence has agreed to swear on an oath that the information they are providing is "the truth, the whole truth, and nothing but the truth". Often, the statement "so help me God" is added at the end of the oath. This relates to those whose biases happen to be religious. This means that they are being watched and recorded, not only by the members of the court, but by a particular supreme being as well. So legally, if a person lies under oath and is caught, they can be charged with perjury and sentenced to serve time in jail. And if they happen to be religious, this would mean that, even though we may not know they are lying, their god will know. And this means that they believe this will affect their lives in some way – possibly through punishment during their current life or perhaps in another life, or an afterlife. Either way, the purpose of testifying under oath is the attempt to assure that the information being provided is truthful, consistent, relevant, reliable, and sufficient.

Intuition

There are also *intuitive* approaches to providing evidence for why we believe what we do. For example, "I didn't walk down that dark alley, because I felt as though it might be dangerous," or "I didn't purchase the car from that salesman, even though it seemed like a great buy, because there was something suspicious about him." These intuitive approaches to evidence come from feelings we might have about specific situations, triggered by cues or behavioral patterns that bring about strong emotional responses in us. Sometimes referred to as *hunches*, they are occasionally right but also quite often wrong. And there seems to be no way to personally regulate these intuitive feelings. What *you* intuitively *feel* might be the exact opposite of what *I'm* intuitively feeling. So who's right and how could we possibly measure this type of evidence? It should come as little surprise then that intuitive evidence is the least justifiable type, due to its unquantifiable nature.

Having said that, there is very interesting developing work in the medical sciences, which examines the relationship between the human stomach and the brain. Known as the "Gut-Brain Connection", scientists at Johns Hopkins, Harvard, and other universities are discovering that our stomachs are really a type of second brain. And there is a direct connection between the biota – the thousands of species of microbes in our stomachs – and the operation of our brains. Both organs can influence each other through the nervous system (e.g. the vagus nerve, as well as the immune system). Known as the "microbiome", our guts house some ten thousand or so species of microbes that are involved in a complex array not only for digestion but also for communication to other systems within the body. So it is possible to imagine that, at some point in the future, scientists might be able to know more about what is going on at the level of our so-called "gut feelings". In this way, the evidence we find compelling through our intuitions, may lie within the realms of the medical sciences.

Scientific Evidence

When we consider scientific evidence, what we are doing is trying to find the best way in which to understand the natural world. In so doing, we present physical or empirical evidence to demonstrate that we are on the right track, in terms of understanding natural properties and mechanisms. As we saw in step one, the type of reasoning called *induction* is one of the hallmarks of scientific investigation. This type of evidence works because when we look at various phenomena in the world – like the effects of gravity – and then observe that they repeatedly occur in the same way under the same conditions over and over again, we can then conclude that they are likely to behave the same way in the future. So this type of evidence satisfies very well the foundational criterion of consistency.

The Scientific Method

Scientific evidence is often obtained by using what has come to be known as the "Scientific Method". Although there is much debate surrounding what the Scientific Method actually is, it can generally be described in the following steps:

1. We initially *observe* a phenomenon of some form.

2. We then make educated guesses called *hypotheses* as to why this phenomenon occurred.

3. We then make *predictions* as to the type of data we should expect to find if our hypothesis is correct.

4. We then proceed to conduct experiments and gather *data*.

5. We are then faced with three possible outcomes:

   a. Either the data gathered supports our prediction and *confirms* our hypothesis.

   b. Or the data gathered fails to support our prediction and *falsifies* our hypothesis.

   c. Or there is *not enough data to determine* one way or the other.

6. Finally, we need to consider if there are any *other competing hypotheses*.

Here's an example of how we might use the Scientific Method: Let's say you were sitting at home and a large branch from a tree crashed through the roof of a house nearby.

1. This is the first step of the scientific method: Your initial *observation* of a phenomenon.

2. In step two, you would consider why this occurred, and in so doing, you would come up with any number of educated guesses or *hypotheses* as to why this happened. For example, it could have been due to a lightning strike. It could have been due to vandalism. It could have been the result of animals living in the tree. It could have been due to termites eating away at the tree. It could have possibly been due to the age of the tree. Or it could have been none of these and was due to a cause we have yet to consider.

3. In the third step, you would make *predictions* about what type of data you would expect to find if one of your hypotheses was correct. If the cause of the fallen tree limb was due to lightning, you would expect to see signs indicating that this was the case. If there was no storm activity that day, this can quickly be ruled out and falsified. If it was due to vandalism, you would expect to find signs of such type of activity. For example, signs of sawing or tampering with the tree limb. If the cause was due to animals living in the tree, you would again expect to see signs of this type of activity (e.g. nests of squirrels, raccoons, etc.). If it was termites, this would easily be detectable by noticing their hollowed out columns within the tree itself, especially around the point at which the branch broke. And finally, if it was due to age, then this would be evident in the physical state of the branch and the tree itself.

4. In step four, you would then proceed to investigate and collect *data* based on your proposed hypotheses and predictions.

5. After collecting data, you will move on to step five and either find that your data supports your prediction and *confirms* one of your hypotheses, or it fails to support your prediction and *falsifies* your hypothesis, or you have *not found enough data* to determine why the tree branch fell through the roof.

6. Remember that you cannot forget step six, which reminds us that there may be an *alternate hypothesis* which could also explain the cause of the

phenomenon. Even if we have attained enough data to support our prediction and confirm a hypothesis, we must always consider other factors that may provide further support as an explanation. For example, that the cause involved not just termites but their activity combined with a very windy day.

In terms of experience and authority, people familiar with the structure of trees, such as arborists, might be brought in as experts to make such a determination. Large tree branches falling on houses is very serious, and we want to be assured that this type of event can be prevented in the future. So we would be well-advised to appeal to the authority of an expert like an arborist, who is far more familiar with trees than the average person, to make such determinations.

This is an ideal situation or example to demonstrate the power of the scientific method. But as critical thinkers, you should know that the process of science is much messier than this and far more politically complex. Many of the topics within both the natural and social sciences are extremely complicated and trying to understand the causal factors behind those complex aspects of nature are extremely difficult. As well, in the last forty years or so, far less attention has been paid to replicating the results of specific experiments. As a result, many studies within various scientific communities go unchallenged and uncorroborated. And this is irresponsible.[10] One meta-study in *Nature* magazine looked at 100 psychological studies and tried to replicate the findings of each study, but could only do so with 39 of them.[11] This gives us some indication of the way in which the scientific community at large has changed in holding itself accountable for methodology and discovery through the peer-review process.

As well, you should also know that the entire political process of science has evolved to a point in which it is very important for institutional scientists

---

10 See: "A manifesto for reproducible science" by Marcus R. Munafò et al, Nature Human Behaviour 1, Articlenumber:0021 (2017) [doi:10.1038/s41562-016-0021].

11 http://www.nature.com/news/over-half-of-psychology-studies-fail-reproducibility-test-1.18248

at universities to be successful, so that they can continue to receive grants, which can bolster the reputation of the university who hired them, to get them the money to be successful, to bolster their reputation, and so on, and so on, *ad nauseam*. Perhaps Richard Smith, former editor of the *British Medical Journal*, said it best when he claimed that most scientific studies are wrong, and they are wrong because scientists are interested in funding and careers rather than truth.[12]

Little attention is paid now to the scientific studies that did not work and the failed discoveries that were never recorded. So much emphasis has been placed on success in confirming hypotheses in science that little attention is being paid to the falsified hypotheses. As a result, this has created an unnecessary imbalance that has perpetuated for decades to only praise and honor the successes. There was a time when scientific failures had far greater value, because they allowed the scientific community to know what avenues *not* to pursue in terms of scientific investigation. And such failed studies are quite valuable, because they can save a lot of time and energy and money. Some efforts are being made to establish databases of failed scientific theories and studies, so that researchers can better understand what works and does not work in the development of specific medicines.[13] If scientists are to be good critical thinkers, they need to know better the context in which they are conducting their investigations. That means they all need to have access to all of the results of all of the studies – not just the successful ones. So please don't think that science is pure and smooth in its operations; it isn't. It's quite messy on a number of levels. The important point to note here is that, in terms of evidence, even with all its faults, it is still the best method for understanding cause-and-effect relationships in the natural world.

---

12 https://www.theguardian.com/science/occams-corner/2013/sep/17/scientific-studies-wrong

13 See: http://retractionwatch.com/

Scientific Studies

Mark Twain once said: "There are three types of lies: lies, damn lies, and statistics."[14] As we have seen with elections in the past, the results of polls and statistics can be accurate or misleading. The majority of information is dependent upon how the polls or studies were conducted, and how the information from them has been interpreted. If you decide to quote studies or polls as evidence to support your premises, you need to consider a number of factors and ask yourself the right questions. There are five very important questions you need to ask whenever anyone – including yourself – uses statistics in support of their premises:

1. Who conducted the study?

2. What was the motivation for the study – in other words, why was it conducted in the first place?

3. Who funded the study?

4. What was the methodology of the study – in other words, how was the study carried out (remember the importance of sample size and representation).

5. Can the study be repeated? That is, would any other scientists, under similar conditions, arrive at the same findings?

There are many examples of various studies that fail to respond to these questions objectively, and therefore are guilty of vested interest or commercial bias. One example that comes to mind was carried out at the University Arizona in 2006. In this particular study, Dr. Charles Gerba compared occupations in order to see which one was the most "germy". His findings concluded that among most professions, teachers and accountants were exposed to the most

---

14 This quote has been attributed to several people including British Prime Minister Benjamin Disraeli but perhaps its most famous reference comes from Mark Twain: Mark Twain's "Chapters from My Autobiography". North American Review (1906-09-07). Project Gutenberg: http://www.gutenberg.org/files/19987/19987.txt.

germs, because of their proximity to keyboards, phones, mouse pads, etc. Personally, I would have thought septic-tank cleaners and waste-management workers might have the "germiest" jobs, but they didn't seem to make the list. Oh well, maybe next year. Anyhow, at first sight, there is nothing overly suspicious about Dr. Gerber's findings. However, when we start to ask some of the five questions, above, we soon find that his research was funded by the good people at Clorox Bleach. And this now leads us to consider what the motivation for the study actually was. The so-called article listing the findings of the study turned out to be a press release sanctioned by the Clorox Bleach Company. And at the very end of the article, there is a paragraph entirely devoted to informing us about the magnificent properties of Clorox disinfecting wipes. So what appears to be a scientifically motivated study, in actuality, is a promotional device used to market and sell a cleaning product. Personally, under specific conditions, I have nothing against the use of bleach as a disinfectant, or the right of Clorox to advertise its products. But when stated in the guise of a scientific study, it lends a level of questionable conduct to the argument and leaves us wondering about the trustworthiness and reliability of the findings.

When we ask questions like the five above, we become immediately empowered with the ability to challenge those who refer to such studies and statistics as evidence in support of their premises for any given argument. So if anyone uses a line like "Studies show that…" in an attempt to support their argument, you have the right to ask them any or all of the above five questions. And likewise, they have the right to do the same to you should you make a similar appeal.

Please keep in mind, however, that scientific studies, when carried out carefully and properly, are still the best means available to us in trying to understand cause and effect relationships in the natural world. We should by no means throw the baby out with the bathwater here. But we must always be careful in considering evidence of any type – including scientific evidence – and be on our guard against the deliberate manipulation of such studies due to vested interest.

E is for evidence. Evidence is important in critical thinking because it allows us to establish facts that add strength to our premises. To be responsible, critical thinkers, we must follow the facts wherever the evidence leads us. To do otherwise would be to do so at our own peril. For example, if I do not believe facts and evidence from the medical sciences that indicate the value of vaccinations in preventing my child from developing measles, pertussis, and meningitis, then I may do so at my child's peril, and my own. In other words, we all have a duty – an obligation – to follow where the facts and evidence leads us. When we ignore evidence and choose to *feel* our way through an issue rather than consider the relevant and reliably obtained facts, then we have abandoned truth and meaning for what Stephen Colbert calls "truthiness".[15] Or as Daniel Moynihan once said: "Everyone is entitled to their own opinion, but not their own facts".[16] And even though we have the right to believe anything we want, we must always be on our guard to assure that, as critical thinkers, we seek out fact-based evidence to the best of our abilities. Otherwise, we may be guilty of committing errors in reasoning known as *"fallacies"*.

---

15 http://www.nytimes.com/2010/10/17/magazine/17FOB-onlanguage-t.html

16 http://www.washingtonpost.com/wp-dyn/content/article/2010/10/01/AR2010100 105262.html

Step 6: F is for Fallacies

We have now ascended five steps towards better thinking. We now know what an argument is; we know how our biases influence how we interpret, consider, and act on information; we have understood why context is so important to information; we possess mental tools which allows us to diagram arguments so that we can better understand their structure; and we are now more aware of the different types of evidence that can be used in supporting our arguments. At this point, we are ready to take the final step, which leads us to consider what aspects or elements might be wrong with an argument. These are called fallacies.

The broad definition of a fallacy is that it is *an error in reasoning*. Basically, there are two types of fallacies: formal and informal. Formal fallacies, as their name implies, deals with errors in their structure or *form*. Informal fallacies deal more with the *content* of the arguments. Our concern lies with the informal type. These are the types of errors in reasoning that people commit every day, often times without even realizing it. In this chapter, we will give specific names to some of the most common errors in reasoning.

If you are to conduct a search online, you would soon learn that there are hundreds of different types of informal fallacies. We are only going to consider some of the most common in alphabetical order.

Ad Hominem

I sometimes refer to this fallacy as the *Sticks and Stones Fallacy*. The term *ad hominem* is Latin and literally means "against the man" or "against the person". This fallacy occurs when we lose focus in our discussion and instead of directing our attack against the content of an argument, we focus instead on irrelevant qualities or characteristics of the person making the argument.

For example, by calling Hilary Clinton a "nasty woman" during a presidential debate, Donald Trump was focusing on irrelevant characteristics rather than dealing with the content of her argument. By calling out Trump on his abilities to manipulate paying taxes or releasing his tax returns, Clinton stated that she wanted to increase taxes – including her own – to help pay for Social Security. As she was stating this, Donald Trump interrupted her by calling her a "nasty woman".

Although it is often tempting to refer to the characteristics of a person that we find personally distasteful, these are never welcomed or warranted in a fair discussion or dialogue about important issues. In fact, an argument is almost immediately lost as soon as a person commits this fallacy. And if you thought the Trump/Clinton debates were heated and filled with *ad hominems (*which they were), recent history reminds us that the principles of proper etiquette in disagreeing and getting along were somewhat abandoned in debates during the Nixon era of the 1960s. One of the most striking examples of abusive *ad hominems* in the history of American twentieth-century debate occurred between Gore Vidal and William F. Buckley Jr.

LET'S GET READY TO *RUMBLE!!!!*

On the evening of Wednesday, Aug. 28, 1968, at 9:39 p.m. on live television, in Chicago at the Democratic National Convention, Gore Vidal – a left-wing, gay, liberal – debated William F. Buckley Jr. – a right wing, extremely not-gay, conservative. The two engaged in one of the most heated political debates of the time. The debate was live and moderated by ABC newsman Howard K. Smith. While discussing America's involvement in the Vietnam

War, and the rights of students to protest the war, the two men became engaged in an extremely heated discussion.

What followed was an emotionally charged series of *ad hominem* attacks, culminating in Buckley's threat to physically beat up Vidal. Here is a portion of their debate:

SMITH: Mr. Vidal, wasn't it a provocative act to try to raise the Vietcong flag in the park in the film we just saw? Wouldn't that invite – raising the Nazi flag during World War II would have had similar consequences.

VIDAL: You must realize what some of the political issues are here. There are many people in the United States who happen to believe that the United States policy is wrong in Vietnam, and the Vietcong are correct in wanting to organize their country in their own way politically. This happens to be pretty much the opinion of Western Europe and many other parts of the world. If it is a novelty in Chicago, that is too bad, but I assume that the point of the American democracy is you can express any point of view you want —

BUCKLEY: (Interrupting) And some people were pro-Nazi.

VIDAL: (Waving hand at Buckley) Shut up a minute.

BUCKLEY: No, I won't. Some people were pro-Nazi, and, and the answer is they were well-treated by people who ostracized them. And I'm for ostracizing people who egg on other people to shoot American Marines and American soldiers. I know you don't care —

VIDAL (loftily): As far as I'm concerned, the only pro- or crypto-Nazi I can think of is yourself. Failing that –

SMITH: Let's, let's not call names –

BUCKLEY (snarling, teeth bared): Now listen, you queer, stop calling me a crypto-Nazi or I'll sock you in your goddamn face, and you'll stay plastered –

(Everybody talks at once. Unintelligible.)

SMITH: Gentlemen!

Buckley and Vidal were arguably two of America's most prominent public intellectuals at the time. And yet both allowed their emotions and their personal attachments to their views get the better of them. You can learn more about their tempestuous relationship in a documentary called: *Best of Enemies*. We all know how difficult it is to maintain control during heated discussions. But as our critical-thinking skills improve, in time, we become better able to resist the temptation to let our more base feelings stand in the way of civil disagreement.

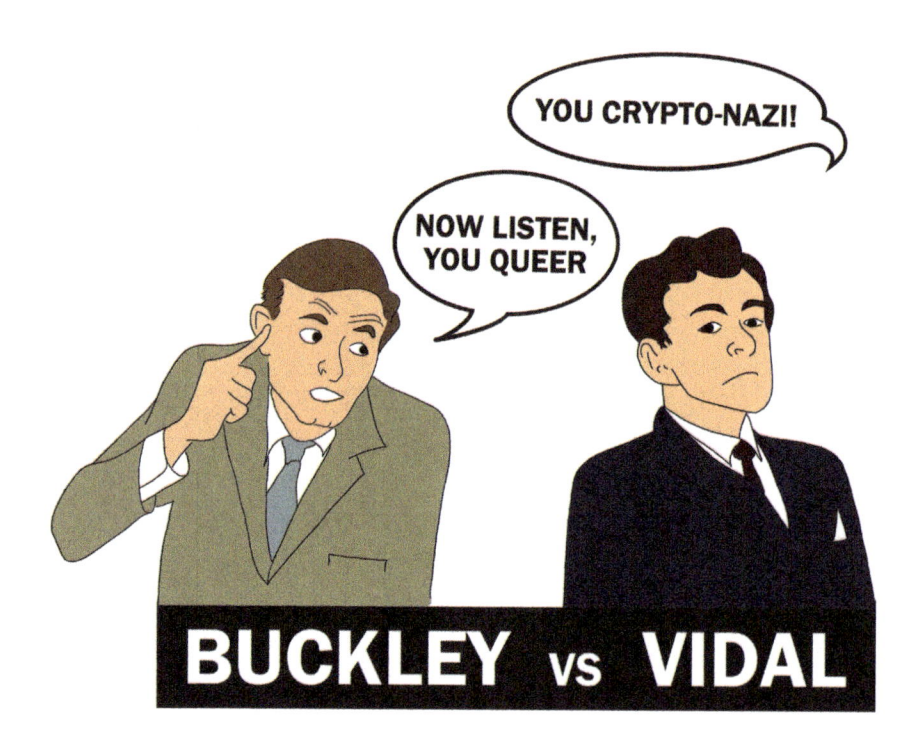

[Illustration: Buckley vs Vidal. Speech bubbles: "NOW LISTEN, YOU QUEER" and "YOU CRYPTO-NAZI!"]

It is interesting how references to Nazis were used between Vidal and Buckley. In the past twenty years or so, it has become quite fashionable for political pundits and various members of the media – especially online – to use *ad hominems* in an effort to demonstrate the severity of their views. What we might call the *Nazi* or *Hitler ad hominem* occurs whenever anyone refers to another person's ideas or actions as similar to those of the Nazi military regime. Barack Obama's administration has been referred to as Nazi-like fascism. George W. Bush has been likened to Hitler. And now, of course, Trump. What's wrong with these types of references is that they tend to overly exaggerate the seriousness of the situation while at the same time trivializing the devastating effects of the Holocaust and the millions who lost their lives during World War II.

An attorney in the United States named Mike Godwin has humorously developed a law which states that "As an online discussion grows longer, the probability of a comparison involving Nazis or Hitler approaches 'one'."[17] So if you've ever been involved in any kind of online discussions, you may have witnessed this first hand. Godwin believes that the longer people discuss particular issues, the greater the likelihood that someone will use an *ad hominem* reference, comparing their ideas to those of Hitler or to Nazis. Known primarily as 'Godwin's Law', it is sometimes referred to as *Argumentum ad Nazium, Reductio ad Hitlerum*, or playing the "Hitler Card".

It's not as though we should never compare the horrific actions of various dictators to those of Hitler. It's just that we need to avoid exaggerations and *ad hominem* attacks so flippantly while discussing important issues. The comedian Jon Stewart said it best: "You know who's like Hitler? Hitler!" So let's keep personal remarks to ourselves and focus on the content of the argument.

Ad Ignorantiam

Also referred to as the "Argument to Ignorance", this could also be called the "*For All You Know Fallacy*". This type of fallacy is committed whenever anyone makes the claim that, *because* someone cannot find complete evidence for the truth of a claim, the claim must be false. Or conversely, since we cannot find complete evidence or proof for the falsity of a claim, it must be true.

If we assume that ghosts or UFOs or psychic abilities exist, because it has not been completely proven that they do not exist, we are fallaciously appealing to this kind of reasoning. You can literally use this type of fallacy to justify just about anything. When children start to question the existence of things like Santa Claus, the Easter Bunny, and the Tooth Fairy, it is all too easy to

---

17 http://rationalwiki.org/wiki/Godwin's_Law.

say to them that their nonexistence has not been proven. And because of this, it means that they *must* exist. Good critical thinkers are vigilant in keeping the burden of proof resting squarely on those who make such claims. Simply because I do not know with 100 percent certainty that all UFO, ghost, and Bigfoot sightings are false, does not necessarily mean that any of them are true. It is the responsibility of those who make such claims to provide the necessary evidence that will lead us to follow their argument to its logical conclusion. Since no such convincing evidence can be presented, we should not be led to believe that such things actually exist. To do so, would be to fall into the trap of appealing to our ignorance. The most common practical example that avoids falling into this trap is in the regulated court system of civilized societies. Here, defendants are *presumed* innocent until proven guilty. Society would commit the fallacy of *Argumentum ad Ignorantiam* if they required the accused to prove their innocence. The burden of proof is kept squarely on the prosecution, who must demonstrate beyond reasonable doubt that the accused is guilty of the crime in question.

Appeal to Authority

We must accept the fact that, due to our limited knowledge, there are many times throughout our daily lives where we must defer or concede to the authority of others. If I'm not feeling well, I see a doctor. I do not go to my mechanic. And if I have car troubles, I do not go to my barber. So there are experts or authorities whom we must seek out in order to attain information, expertise, and the proper services. The appeal to authority only becomes a fallacy when we do so to a particular individual or group whose authority on the topic at hand is questionable.

"I was driving a Lincoln long before I got paid to drive a Lincoln," says Matthew McConaughey. So we should purchase one too, right? Matthew McConaughey is a very good actor, but what do his acting abilities have to do with his authority in recommending good automobiles to purchase? The same holds true for any celebrity who endorses any product. Their fame and stature as recognized celebrities in no way makes them authorities on any particular topic – I'm looking at you, Jenny McCarthy. The authority I seek out for information regarding vaccinations comes from the World Health Organization, the Center for Disease Control, and hundreds upon hundreds of peer-reviewed research papers from notable scientists, microbiologists, disease specialists, epidemiologists, etc., in order to better understand information about vaccinations, how they work, and their possible side effects. That's because, when it comes to factual knowledge and information about inoculation procedures, they are the best authorities. I do not seek out the authority of an actress who has virtually no understanding of how vaccinations actually function.

Please keep in mind that an argument's strength stands on the solidity of its premises, and how well those premises satisfy the universal foundational criteria – not simply on who endorses that argument. And so proper appeals to authority are always secondary to the premises contained within an argument and the evidence supplied in support of those premises.

Ad Populum or Appeal to Popularity

This is also known as the *"Bandwagon Fallacy"*. The phrase "jumping on the bandwagon" is a slang reference used to designate somebody who only recently started agreeing with popular opinion. That opinion could be anything from the support of a local sports team that is doing well in the playoffs, to a new idea or meme that is circulating around the Internet, or the office, or the household. There is no guarantee that the popularity of an idea is an indication of its truth. It was popular at one point in time to believe that the world was flat and that the sun revolved around the world. But those days are gone – with the exception of the Cleveland Cavaliers' Kyrie Irving and a few other NBA players.[18] And those days are gone largely because we developed a better understanding of the way in which the natural world actually works. So the popularity of an idea in no way guarantees its truth. Proper reasoning, correct inferences, strong premises adhering to foundational criteria, and not committing fallacies or errors in reasoning, are what strengthens an argument or an idea. At various times throughout

---

18 I sincerely hope this is a hoax. As publication of this book approaches, it appears that Shaquille O'Neal has now joined and since rescinded his flat-earth theory claiming he was joking.

history, people popularly justified slavery, forced prostitution, child labor, human battles to the death, and so on. Simply because they were popular, and accepted at one point in time, does not necessarily make them right.

There are, however, cases in which the popularity of ideas contributes to its justification. We find these in particular fields of scientific expertise. Within many of the sciences, there exists a level of professionalism in which peer members monitor the work of others, and over time, a consensus of understanding occurs in which specific ideas will receive a majority of approval. And so there is a consensus of opinion within the natural sciences who accept Einstein's theories of relativity, and this acceptance has gained considerably in popularity. But it is important to understand that Einstein's theories did not gain acceptance because they became popular; they became popular because they were widely accepted and could be confirmed through the six steps of the scientific method that we saw in the previous chapter.

As a collective of authorities within a given field, any appeal to strongly held ideas by a group of such people is not a fallacious appeal to popularity, because the ideas to which they subscribe have gained in popularity *because* they have satisfied the criteria of scientific and logical rigor. Eventually, those with authority recognize such ideas, subscribe to them, and then they become popular within a particular group of authorities and throughout the non-scientific community. But remember, as in the case with Einstein's theories of relativity, he did all of the hard work first, and *then* people began to subscribe to it. The theory stands on its own without the need of anyone's consent. The popularity of it came after physicists started to realize how relevant and accurate it was.

Begging the Question

This fallacy involves a form of *Circular Reasoning*. It occurs whenever any premise assumes the truth of the conclusion instead of supporting it. Consider the following examples:

> My psychic must have the gift of clairvoyance because only someone with clairvoyance could have known that I visited my grandmother in Belgium last summer.
>
> The reason why this car is so popular is because everybody wants one.

Even if the conclusions were true, the premises do not support the conclusions – they assume them. These arguments move in a circular fashion, so that the conclusions support the premises which in turn support the conclusions. The premises "beg the question" by assuming or stating the truth of the conclusion as support. *Jane is a good dancer, because she dances well.* This circular argument begs the question of whether or not she actually dances well, passing it over and assuming the truth of the conclusion as though it is already established fact, when it is not.

As a warning, be aware that, for about the last twenty years or so, the term "begging the question" has been used improperly by journalists. It is difficult to determine who first began the misuse, but it's become quite fashionable to use it as a hipster catch-phrase. Consider the following improper use of the term:

> Reporter: I'm currently standing outside of the collapsed building. The destruction is severe and the casualty rates are high; it appears to have been built improperly, which begs the question: "How could this have happened?"

In this case, the reporter should have said that it *raises* the question, or *poses*, or *suggests*, or *invites* the question … not *begs* the question. "Begs the question" is a phrase specifically related to circular reasoning.

I still hear the phrase used incorrectly from time to time by journalists and news anchors. It's a sort of sexy, hip way of incorrectly referring to information. I came across an interesting site called: Beg the Question: Get it Right.[19]

---

19 http://begthequestion.info/

The hosts of this site and its followers are attempting to bring attention to the proper use of this informal logical fallacy and to issue cards of notice to those who use it improperly.

So let's be careful when restating our premises, so that they do not assume the very thing we are trying to support. Otherwise, we would be begging the question.

Disanalogy

I sometimes refer to this fallacy as the *Apples and Oranges Fallacy*. It is perfectly normal to make comparisons when we're trying to state a point. When analogies are properly used, they are extremely helpful in getting people to understand a particular concept, an opinion, or a point of view. However, sometimes we don't always choose good analogies. And when this is the case, we need to know why the comparison is not a good one. Consider the following example:

> Too many kids these days are consuming far too much soda. They are hooked on the stuff just like junkies are hooked on crystal meth.

The question we need to ask ourselves now is this: How similar and dissimilar is the consumption of soda to the use of a highly addictive drug such as crystal methamphetamine? If the two are far more dissimilar than they are similar, then one is guilty of committing the fallacy of disanalogy.

There are many analogies that have been used throughout history. One might say that most of literature involves analogies with extended metaphors, symbolic comparisons, and so on. From Shakespeare's lines: "Shall I compare thee to a summer day?" to Forest Gump's statement that: "Life is like a box of chocolates", it would be very difficult for us to be able to navigate through this world without the use of comparisons with analogies. And so, just as the majestic bald eagle carefully chooses upon which branches to build its nest, so must you be just as selective in choosing analogies to support your arguments.

Equivocation

This fallacy is caused whenever someone uses a term, or phrase, or sentence in an argument with two different meanings. For example:

(P1) Power corrupts.
(P2) Knowledge is power.
(C) Therefore, knowledge corrupts.

In the first premise, the use of the word "power" means political power and hence, one's inherent weakness that possessing power will corrupt them to the point of abusing that position of power for personal gain – sort of like possessing a ring of invisibility. Precious…

In the second premise, the word "power" refers to the ability of humans to be able to understand the natural world, and in so doing, become empowered to use that understanding to our betterment.

During any discussion, the fallacy of equivocation can arise if we engage in a verbal rather than a genuine dispute. With verbal disputes, we are guilty of each using a term differently. For example, if a groundskeeper at a golf course told me he was going to kill all the gophers on the course, and I thought he said "golfers",[20] we would be dealing with two completely different issues. In order for there to be a genuine dispute, we must be referring to the same issue. Consider another popular example:

P1: Nothing is better than eternal happiness.
P2: A of bowl of soup is better than nothing.
C1: A bowl of soup is better than eternal happiness.

A popular example of the fallacious use of equivocation arises around the debates, conversations, and dialogues that people have about creationism versus evolution. What I find somewhat troubling is the manner in which some people will claim that evolutionary theory should not be taken very

---

20 Thank you, *Caddyshack*.

seriously, because it is, after all, "just a theory" – I'm looking at you, U.S. Vice President Mike Pence.

What they fail to realize is that they are equivocating on the word "theory". They are not using the word "theory" in the same manner as scientists use it (e.g. the theory of gravity, quantum theory, etc.), which comes from the Greek word "*theoria*", meaning a natural explanation of some aspect of the world, which has been strongly supported by evidence. Instead, they are using the word to mean less certain mental states, like "hunch" or "guess" or "conjecture". And this is unfair. Part of the problem may come from a simple misunderstanding. While doing a quick, basic online search for the word "theory", I found these two definitions directly beside each other:

Theory:

> 1. A coherent group of general propositions used as principles of explanation for a class of phenomena: Einstein's theory of relativity. Synonyms: principle, law, doctrine.
>
> 2. A proposed explanation whose status is still conjectural, in contrast to well-established propositions that are regarded as reporting matters of actual fact. Synonyms: idea, notion hypothesis, postulate.[21]

The great majority of those within the scientific community will identify that the way in which scientists use the word "theory" is that found in the first definition, above. Whereas those who tend to equivocate on the use of the term "evolutionary theory", most often choose the definition found in the second definition.

No matter which side of the debate we come down upon, whether they deal with the most mundane or the loftiest of topics, we must always be on our guard to make sure that we interpret terms, words, and phrases in the manner which best represents their intentions. Otherwise, we may be guilty of equivocation and unfairly slow the progress of meaningful dialogue.

---

21 http://www.dictionary.com/browse/theory

False Dilemma

This could also be called the *"Black or White Fallacy"*, because it assumes that there are only two choices, sides, or alternatives, when in fact there are more – perhaps fifty or more shades of gray. Whenever people state that there are two and only two approaches to a particular topic, if you can demonstrate a third, or fourth, or fiftieth, then you have demonstrated how that person has committed the fallacy of false dilemma.

You should also know, however, that there are genuine dilemmas. Sometimes in life, there really are just two alternatives.

For example:

> There's no such thing as being a little bit pregnant.
>
> When you die, your consciousness will either continue or it will not.
>
> Either the universe had a beginning or it did not.

So a genuine dilemma does not admit to degrees between extremes. But false dilemmas can be demonstrated by stating alternatives to the proposed extremes.

> In my view, a person is basically entirely good or completely evil.
>
> Either you are totally a Democrat or you are totally a Republican.
>
> To stop the massive number of concussions in American football games, we must ban the sport!

In each case, it should be noted that the speaker wrongly implies that the list of choices is complete. In the first case, a person's behavior could never be classified as being entirely good or entirely evil. All people are generally a mixture of different types of behaviors. But I know of no human being who has ever been entirely good or entirely evil. And so I believe this statement to commit the fallacy of false dilemma.

In the second case, a person does not simply have to be either a Democrat or Republican. Not only are there other candidates from other parties that one could choose, one can also be a right-leaning Democrat or left-leaning Republican. Thus the category of *centrist* emerges. So there are quite a few other choices or shades of gray available in terms of political affiliations and loyalties.

And in the final case, it's not as though we don't think concussions are bad, it's just that we don't want players to continue to suffer. But is banning the sport the *only* solution? A third possibility might involve changing rules about head contact, specific types of violent tackling, and other forms of contact that are likely to generate concussive effects. So, to say that either the sport continues or it must be banned is to commit the fallacy of false dilemma.

When people present ideas that indicate that there are only two choices available, we need to be aware that they might not be genuine but instead stating false dilemmas. It is easy to assume that various aspects of the world can be neatly polarized in this way. It may also give the false impression that the speaker has done some research, i.e., that after careful consideration, it appears that there *are* only two alternatives: A or B. Be wary of this when doctors tell you that there are only two possible outcomes available: the treatment they suggest or the harmful effects of the ailment. You should know that there is often more than just one treatment for any given ailment and sometimes you need to ask for a second opinion to determine which treatment might be best for you.

__Hasty Generalization__

This can also be referred to as the *"Jumping to Conclusions Fallacy"*. This fallacy is committed when one reaches a conclusion without sufficient premises. So this fallacy occurs when the foundational criterion of sufficiency is not satisfied by the premises. This error in reasoning is most clearly seen when people make generalizations from an insufficient number of particular events. For example, a great deal of discrimination is the result of hastily concluding generalized or broad conclusions that unfairly treats all members of a group the same due to the behavior of a few. Just as it would be a hasty generalization to believe that, with the occurrences of racial tension in the U.S., all young black men are potential thugs and criminals, so equally would one commit the fallacy of a hasty generalization in believing that all police officers are racially biased and motivated. The root causes of hasty generalizations are often found in fear, ignorance, prejudice, and other biases, which can often lead us to make quick or rash judgments. Hasty generalizations are drawn because we have been convinced of a conclusion before a sufficient amount of evidence or premises has been gathered.

The danger of making hasty generalizations becomes painfully clear in other areas as well such as the field of medicine. Past historical accounts show clearly why it is so important to gather a sufficient amount of premises before reaching a conclusion. The drug thalidomide (commonly distributed as Immunoprin, Distaval, and Contergan) was used worldwide during the 1950s and 60s to treat various ailments, such as mild insomnia, anxiety, and morning sickness in pregnant women. It worked. However, for expectant mothers, it caused severe deformations of the developing fetuses and thousands of children were born with underdeveloped arms and legs. It took five years before an Australian gynecologist, Dr. William McBride, made the connection between thalidomide and the effects of deformed limbs with newborns. This discovery led not only to hundreds of lawsuits, but also to the introduction of tougher regulations for testing, licensing, and reclassifying drugs.[22]

Meanwhile, in 1964, an Israeli physician named Jacob Sheskin was desperately trying to control the pain of many of his patients who were suffering from the skin lesions and boils caused by leprosy. Fearing he had no other alternatives to minimize their pain, he administered doses of thalidomide, so that they could at least sleep. To everyone's great surprise, by the next day, all of their skin lesions had disappeared.

And today, thalidomide is being used to treat specific types of cancers. In 1993, Judah Folkman pioneered work in the successful treatment of specific types of blood cancers, known as multiple myeloma, by administering thalidomide. Within six years, clinical trials and numerous journal articles demonstrated the efficacy of using thalidomide in treating multiple myeloma. By 2006, the FDA approved the use of thalidomide in combination with dexamethasone for cancer patients suffering from multiple myeloma.

So medical history has demonstrated that we must be careful in making hasty generalizations. In the initial use of thalidomide, the generalization was made that it was an excellent drug in the treatment of a number of ailments, including morning sickness in women. Then it was discovered that thalidomide contributed to thousands of deformed babies and so the generalization was made that it should not be used in the treatment of morning sickness. But such a generalization did not stop further consideration of the possible positive effects of such a drug. And thankfully, for thousands of patients suffering from leprosy and multiple myeloma, the generalization did not include them.

---

22 For example, the Directive 65/65/EEC1 (Europe) and the Kefauver Harris Amendment (U.S.). Stricter rules were developed and enforced in the U.S. by the FDA that required evidence indicating the effectiveness of drugs and statements as to whether any side effects were detected during testing. This led to the Drug Efficacy Study Implementation, which retroactively reclassified drugs that were on the shelves at the time.

As we saw in step five, it is not always easy to know when enough evidence has been gathered in order to make a reasoned assessment of a claim. We must realize that evidence in some areas will be more sufficient than in others. But we still need to keep asking the important questions in order to avoid arriving at generalizations too hastily.

Post Hoc Fallacy

The term "post hoc" is a Latin phrase meaning "after this". The entire name of the fallacy is actually *"post hoc ergo propter hoc"*, which means "after this, therefore, because of this". Normally referred to as a "post-hoc fallacy", this occurs when someone assumes that, because A precedes B, A *must* be the cause of B. Consider the following examples:

Example 1: Every year during the NHL hockey playoffs, many players grow beards for good luck. When a team wins the Stanley Cup, many of the players have beards. It follows then, that their growing beards caused them to win the NHL championship.

In this case, it is not the act of growing beards that causes the team to win the championship. The team that happens to play the best and score the most goals will win the coveted Stanley Cup. There were plenty of other teams whose players grew beards and yet none of them won the Stanley Cup.

Example 2: We should re-activate World War II air raid sirens in our city to signal when tornadoes have been spotted in the area. Shelbyville did this ten years ago, and they haven't seen a tornado since.

In this case, the person has mistakenly believed that because no tornadoes have occurred after the air-raid sirens were activated, it follows that it must be the re-activation of the sirens that was the cause of the decline of tornado activity. The actual reason for the lack of tornadoes may be due to coincidence, or chance, or simply the lack of turbulent weather.

Example 3: In an episode from *The Simpsons*, a wandering bear comes into the city of Springfield. The citizens establish a Bear Patrol to keep bears out of the city. Homer tells his daughter, Lisa, that since no bears have been seen, the patrol committee must be doing a good job. Lisa responds by saying that Homer's reasoning is specious. She says it is similar to saying that the rock she is holding is responsible for keeping tigers out of Springfield. By the same reasoning Homer used, she says that since no tigers have been seen, it must be due to the rock. Homer wants to purchase the rock.

What Homer fails to realize but Lisa clearly sees is that it is not the patrol committee that is keeping the bears out of Springfield. It is because there are simply no bears around – there was only the one isolated incident. So the cause of the lack of bears is not due to the patrol committee but to the fact that there simply are no more bears wandering into Springfield.

Example 4: What is the likelihood of my being in a car accident wearing a clown suit when I drive on Highway 401? It's pretty close to zero. Therefore, whenever I drive on the 401, shouldn't I always wear a clown suit?[23]

If I were to drive on a major highway in a clown suit and did not get into a car accident, it would not be the suit that has kept me safe on my travels. It would be my abilities as a competent driver, fair weather, low traffic volume, luck, etc.

---

23 This is example is taken from an old friend and past professor of mine, Bill Hughes.

Six Steps to Better Thinking

In each case, we can see how prior occurrences are not the actual causes for the eventual effects. The Post Hoc fallacy is often committed using hasty generalizations and anecdotal evidence. One of the most famous examples of this fallacy involves the claims of model/actress Jenny McCarthy that specific childhood vaccines cause autism. Ms. McCarthy witnessed her son experiencing signs associated with autism *after* he was vaccinated. And so she mistakenly believed that the order of the events pointed directly to the singular cause of her son's vaccination. Unfortunately, the premises of her argument were extremely weak and were unable to satisfy the foundational criteria of consistency, relevance, reliability, and sufficiency. As well, there is very little scientific evidence supporting Ms. McCarthy's claim. It follows then, that it would be more responsible to believe that the causes of her son's autism were due to other factors. If at some point in the future, evidence can

99

be produced demonstrating a causal connection between vaccinations and autism, then we would have to follow where that evidence leads us. However, this has not been the case. Irrespective of the overwhelming amount of evidence for the safety and benefit of vaccinations, many parents in the United States have chosen not to have their children vaccinated. As a result, many incidents of diseases have risen and led to a considerable amount of sickness, discomfort, and in some cases, even the death of children.[24] In learning how to think about important issues, and how to disagree and get along, this is a very difficult topic to discuss because children's lives are at stake. But as with all matters in critical thinking, we must follow the facts wherever the evidence leads us.

Red Herring

This could also be called the *"Something Smells Fishy Fallacy"*. This fallacy occurs whenever one states a premise or premises that are not relevant to the conclusion and intentionally tries to distract attention away from the topic at hand. In this way, one shifts the topic so that the focus is no longer on the originally stated issue. To get a better understanding of what a Red Herring Fallacy is, consider the following analogy: Imagine that a prisoner has escaped from jail and the guards are tracking him with bloodhounds which are picking up his scent as he runs through the forest. He knows that he will eventually be caught, because his scent will lead the dogs right to his location. However, our clever prisoner has a large smelly fish with him, which he borrowed from the cafeteria. He drags the fish behind him as he runs through the forest, and as the dogs come across the smell of the fish, they lose his scent and so the prisoner escapes. In the same manner, when people commit Red Herring Fallacies, they're trying to throw us off of their scent, as it were, in the hopes that they can escape being held accountable for their beliefs or actions. Red herrings work very well in murder mysteries. We often suspect one character or another and the plot development leads us

---

24 http://www.cidrap.umn.edu/news-perspective/2016/03/study-relates-vaccine-refusal-rise-measles-pertussis

to rethink who the actual murderer might be. Unfortunately, they also work quite well for politicians. Consider the following excellent example from an episode of *Family Guy*, in which townspeople are asking mayoral candidates about specific policies:

Mort Goldman: "Mayor West, if elected, would you increase the frequency of garbage pickup?"

Mayor West: "Well citizen, that's an excellent question and I thank you for it. I think it's great we live in a town where you can ask questions. Because without questions, we just have answers. And an answer without a question is just a statement."

Mort Goldman: "Oh, I like him. He looks me in the eye."[25]

It's clear that Mayor West's response has nothing to do with whether or not the frequency of garbage pickup will be increased. Mort Goldman has fallen for the charm of a candidate using a red herring, which has distracted him away from the topic at hand. In the political satire movie called *The Campaign*, the comedian Zach Galifianakis referred to his political opponent's red herring response to a debate question as the "DC dip and twirl" maneuver.

Whatever name it happens to go by, the Red Herring Fallacy is usually the deliberate attempt by a person or organization to avoid directly responding to a specific question. By far, one of the most famous (and obvious) red herrings took place during the murder trial of O.J. Simpson. Mr. Simpson's defense team – led by Johnny Cochrane – stated that O.J. was framed for multiple homicides because of collective racial hatred, at several levels of police and forensic investigation, within the LAPD. Johnny Cochrane was extremely successful at diverting the jury's attention away from the hard facts of the case and had them preoccupied with the incredibly unlikely possibility that O.J. Simpson was framed because of racial hatred.

---

25 Family Guy: 'It Takes a Village Idiot and I Married One'. Season 5, Episode 17. Production No: 5ACX12. First aired: May 13, 2007.

In the case of the O.J. Simpson trial, the entire world was watching it on CNN for over two years. There was an overwhelming amount of evidence implicating O.J. Simpson as the murderer of Nicole Brown Simpson and Ronald Goldman. However the LAPD *was* involved in numerous beatings of black men – the most public being that of Rodney King. Millions of people, including myself, did not want to believe that O.J. Simpson could kill two people. However, the evidence suggested otherwise. The jurors should have followed where the evidence led them: to a verdict of guilty on both counts of murder. But the jurors were swept up by the brilliant defense tactics of Johnny Cochrane, who played the race card to the great benefit of his client, and in so doing, the entire world witnessed what was arguably the greatest red herring in the history of American justice. As entertaining as Mr. Simpson's trial was, we must never forget that two people were brutally murdered, and a man got away with murder, as the entire world watched the jury ignore the most important evidence of the case and instead chose to follow an elaborate and very well-presented red herring.

So please be fair in your discussions and answer questions truthfully without the willful intent to mislead. If everyone avoided such tactics, we would all be better off.

<u>The Slippery Slope Fallacy</u>

To better understand the meaning of this fallacy, imagine that you are standing at the top of a hill that is very icy. As soon as you begin to walk down the hill, you will not be able to stop. No matter how hard you try, you will not be able to go back up the hill, and you will inevitably slide down it until you reach the bottom. So too, with the Slippery Slope Fallacy, will people argue against a particular action because they believe that once started, it will inevitably lead to an unavoidably bad result.

So the slippery slope is a metaphor for a chain of causal events. Once a single cause starts, it will create an effect that will be the cause of another effect, and so on, until the final effect results in something really terrible. As a metaphor, the slippery slope describes the compounding effect or long-term consequences of our actions, so that once we get started, we may not be able to stop. Many of us will have experienced either using or hearing someone use this form of reasoning at some point in our lives. There is the classic warning: Smoking pot is simply a "gateway drug", which will invariably lead you to try uppers, downers, LSD, mushrooms, PCP, cocaine, heroin, etc. These actions will lead you to become a drug addict, who will be forced to steal and rob people in order to support your habit; eventually, you will either end up in jail or die. And all because of one shtick of the stuff.[26] To be fair, there have been people who have followed this exact path down their own slippery slopes – people like Jim Morrison, Janis Joplin, Jimi Hendrix, Kurt Cobain, etc. But this does not mean that every person who tries marijuana will inevitably slide down the slope and die. There are millions of people who smoke pot and maintain fairly active, healthy lives without ever having moved on to harder drugs. Or perhaps they did harder drugs, and now just smoke pot. Or don't use any substances at all. Surely, the continued existence of Keith Richards must prove this. We can identify when a person is guilty of committing the Slippery Slope Fallacy whenever we can demonstrate that simply by starting at the top of the slope, does not necessarily mean that the events will inevitably lead to the bottom of it.

One of the most common examples in recent history that references the slippery slope is the debate that exists regarding euthanasia, or mercy killing, or doctor-assisted death.[27] Allowing a person to make a decision regarding their end-of-life care is liberating for some people and quite distressing for others. This will be one of the topics we consider in the next chapter, but for right now, our concern is with the manner in which the slippery slope metaphor has been used in popular dialogue recently. Those who do not favor assistance in dying often cite the possibility that by allowing terminally ill patients the power to end their lives, this will generate more frequent usage of this method for end-of-life care for less and less severe medical ailments. So today

---

26 Thank you Joe Flaherty.

27 Since 2016, in Canada, this is now referred to as medical assistance in dying (MAID).

we euthanize for stage IV terminal cancer; next year, we euthanize for people suffering from AIDS; the year after that, we euthanize for stroke; and so on and so on until little by little, we find ourselves euthanizing people simply because they were having a bad hair day. All joking aside, we need to take into consideration to what extent a slippery slope regarding euthanasia could become a reality. And to assure that committees are put in place to assure that a slide down such a slope does not occur in the future.

__Strawman Fallacy__

This can also be referred to as the *"Caricature Fallacy"*. As I've been saying repeatedly throughout this book, fairness is the *Cornerstone of Critical Thinking*. If we all play by the rules fairly, this may not guarantee that there will be less disagreement, but it will greatly increase the likelihood of being understood. If we misrepresent another person's argument, whether intentionally or not, and then address the misunderstanding of that argument, we create a caricature of the argument – something neither real nor intended.

The strawman metaphor has been used for decades, because its name references the straw men that were sometimes constructed during times of war preparation, in order to give the military trainees a practice target. So the military are not attacking real men but constructed or fake men. The same holds for strawman arguments. If we misinterpret a person's argument – whether intentionally or not – and then proceed to critique it, this misinterpretation will invariably lead to an irrelevant commentary, because we would be guilty of not faithfully representing the intention of the argument. We owe it to ourselves and others to faithfully establish their intended position and support for it. This obligation is simply part of what it means to be fair in critical thinking.

In both congress and the senate, the committing of Strawman Fallacies wastes considerable time, energy, and money. And this is because everything that is said about a misrepresented argument has no relevance. We have taken the intentions of their argument and misconstrued them to create a caricature, or fake, or unintended strawman argument. We must be vigilant in representing our opponent's arguments in their best possible light. To do otherwise, would be unfair, and something that – according to the *Golden Rule of Dialogue* – we, ourselves, would not want. Therefore, we ought not to do this. And when we avoid committing such fallacies, we will have grown and most assuredly made it to the final step to better thinking.

F is for Fallacies. We have considered thirteen of the most common fallacies that people commit every day. We should take considerable care to recognize such errors of reasoning not only in the views of others, but especially in our own. By avoiding such fallacies, we can go a long way towards successful and meaningful dialogue.

There are better and worse ways to think about issues. We have covered the six most essential steps to becoming better thinkers and engaging in fair and intelligent discussions. And as we now turn our thoughts to consider specific controversial topics, we will see how these steps can help us in facilitating meaningful dialogue and establishing common ground, in an effort to alleviate or soften disagreement.

How to Disagree and Get Along

Now that you know what the six steps are and how to use them, it will become increasingly easy to have important and sometimes heated discussions about controversial issues and still get along. As I mentioned earlier, agreeing and getting along is easy. Disagreeing and getting along requires the continued and consistent use of the six steps. But like anything worth pursuing, this takes time and practice. Here are the ways in which we can use the six steps to disagree and get along:

1. A is for Argument.

The first thing that needs to be done is to establish *what* each other is saying in the best possible light. In other words, what are the arguments – yours and theirs? In establishing your intended argument and trying to establish that of another, be sure to practice *fairness:* the *Cornerstone of Critical Thinking*. Make every effort to state the other person's argument in the best possible light of intent. You would expect the same from them. This is what was referred to as the *Golden Rule of Dialogue.* After you have indicated that you sufficiently understand the intent of the person with whom you are having a dialogue, and have been able to demonstrate this by stating it back to them, you can now proceed to discussing the value of their argument. There may be some aspects to which you agree, and others which you oppose. Determine first the positive aspects of the argument and any and all common points where you agree. Be sure to initially offer constructive prior to destructive criticism.

2. B is for Bias.

When the time comes for you to state the premises of the argument with which you disagree, do so in a manner that clearly indicates why it is that someone with *your* particular set of biases would disagree, and why it is that someone with *their* particular set of biases might choose such premises in support of their conclusion. What biases might be involved on both sides of the issue? Make every effort to understand both the biological and cultural biases that have given rise to the differences of viewpoints you each have. And then consider how both of your sets of biases have led to the current dispute or disagreement. Also, consider how you might understand the issue differently if your biases developed differently. For example, would you still think about an issue the same way if you had grown up 10,000 miles away in a country very much different from your own?

3. C is for Context.

Have both of you considered and interpreted the information according to the proper context of the issue? Pay particular attention to the three major components of context – time, place, and circumstance – and understand that information does not exist in a vacuum, but is always situated within a specific context. Ensure that you are fully aware of the 'back story'. Make sure that you have interpreted their premises in as fair a context as possible. Otherwise, you run the risk of misinterpretation and creating a strawman out of their argument. And as we have seen, any critique against such an unintended argument is worthless and demonstrates unfairness on your part. Fairly representing the context in which the information was housed will save all parties time, energy, and money.

4. D is for Diagram.

What do both of your arguments look like? Try to imagine the structure of their argument in your mind. Imagine their conclusion as the roof, and what their supporting premises as walls would look like. And then consider to what extent their premises managed to satisfy or failed to satisfy the universal foundational criteria of consistency, simplicity, reliability, relevance, and sufficiency. If you have the time, you can diagram them in a fair and respectful manner, to faithfully interpret and represent the intention of each other's argument. This again draws upon the *Golden Rule of Dialogue,* i.e. representing another's argument with the same manner of intent as you would want for your own.

5. E is for Evidence.

What type(s) of evidence were offered, if any? Determine the type of evidence and the manner in which it supports or fails to support the premises. Constructively state why you believe the evidence is acceptable or not. If purely anecdotal evidence was offered, you can point out that you can understand why such an experience has had such an impact upon a person. However, you can also point out that singular personal experiences do not always provide the type of support required for such a conclusion. And this is due to a lack of statistically significant data that would collectively support their premises. If intuitive evidence is offered, you can mention that intuitions are sometimes right, but often wrong. And if scientific evidence is offered, determine the source and the reliability of the findings. Consider the six stages of the scientific method, and determine if the findings were arrived at through such a rigorous process. If evidence from scientific studies is offered, consider the five important questions from step five. And always remember the Sagan Principle: Extraordinary claims require extraordinary evidence. So hold people accountable for their claims. And don't be afraid to ask for the appropriate type of evidence in support of their claims. Otherwise, why should you be convinced of their argument? If the evidence is weak and does not satisfy the universal foundational criteria, then the premises cannot stand, and the conclusion (roof) will come crashing down.

6. F is for Fallacies.

As we saw in step six, there are many different types of fallacies. It becomes easier to spot them with practice. If any fallacies were committed, name them and demonstrate how they were committed. Remember, just because fallacies may have been committed, it does not mean that the entire argument itself is bad or unwarranted. We may not need to throw the baby out with the bathwater as they say. Few (if any) arguments are perfect. Critical thinking allows us to constructively contribute to the development, revision, and support of ideas, including those with which we disagree.

> For those interested in pursuing the practical applications of the six steps, you will find exercises, feedback, videos, and commentary at: www.sixstepstobetterthinking.com.

After using the six steps, determine the points of agreement and commonality to better understand why disagreement is not a sufficient defense for incivility, hatred, or violence. Now let's turn our attention towards the discussion of six important but controversial issues which are often emotionally charged and generate considerable disagreement.

Discussing Controversial Issues: Disagreeing and Getting Along

As a young man, my mother warned me about the dangers of discussing specific topics in diverse public settings. "Christopher," she would say, "when in mixed company, one should never discuss religion, sex, or politics."

"But momma," I would say, "that's where the fun is."[28]

We know there are "hot button" or controversial topics and issues which almost immediately lead to heated discussions. However, one of the reasons why these topics are so controversial is because they are so important to our everyday lives, and we are very much emotionally attached to them. But that's why it is so important to be able to have meaningful dialogues about them, and have the freedom by which to disagree, but at the same time still be able to get along with one another. We are going to briefly consider six

---

28 Thanks, Bruce.

controversial topics to discuss: euthanasia, abortion, gun control, capital punishment, same-sex relationships, and religion. For each topic, I will state the polar opposite viewpoints. You can then better situate yourself either at one end or the other or somewhere along the spectrum between these two extreme polarized viewpoints. We will then look at some common ground that exists between each point of disagreement in an effort to demonstrate how each side can continue to disagree and still get along.

(i) Euthanasia: Physician Assisted Dying (PAD) or Medical Assistance in Dying (MAID) - For/Against

The Extreme Polar Views:

For Euthanasia: We should allow all citizens during any point in their illness – regardless of the severity of their condition – the right to decide when and how they wish to be humanely put to death.

Against Euthanasia: We should never allow any citizen under any circumstance to have their lives ended intentionally. We must do everything in our medical power to keep a person alive for as long as possible.

On which side of this debate do you tend to fall? And why? What would your argument look like? How carefully have you thought about this particular topic? If you believe that euthanasia should never be allowed no matter what the circumstances, what has led you to have this current viewpoint? And the same holds for those who believe people should be allowed to have their lives ended through medical assistance. What we tend to find when discussing these issues is the level to which personal biases play a part in formulating our thoughts and acting on those beliefs. Some people base their disagreement with euthanasia on religious grounds. If that's the case, why might a person currently have a specific religious perspective that disallows them from accepting personal control over end-of-life care? And for those who wish to allow people the capacity to control how they wish to die, what evidence or premises have they developed in support of this conclusion?

Some people in the U.S. have argued that in allowing for the opportunity to discuss end-of-life care, in considering the possibility of assisted euthanasia, there will be so-called "death panels", which will execute Grandma at the first sign of a cold. As we saw in step six, this particular viewpoint commits the fallacy of the slippery slope. This viewpoint maintains that, over time, less and less terminal illnesses will be sufficient grounds to allow people to end their lives. So it may start with stage IV terminal cancer, but over time will be used for less severe illnesses. The fear of the slippery slope with euthanasia is that, once it becomes legalized for people with terminal illnesses, eventually the laws will become more and more relaxed and we will be inclined to euthanize people with non-life-threatening diseases, or that many will simply give up their desire to live and rush to the hospitals to be "put down".

But where does the actual evidence lead us? So far, in the U.S., physician aid in dying (PAD), or assisted suicide, is legal in California, Colorado, Oregon, Vermont, and Washington. And in all states, the reports indicate that terminally ill people considering such an option do not always choose euthanasia – even when it is legally accessible. In fact, in Oregon from 1998 to 2002, only 129 people opted for physician-assisted death. So it does not appear that a slippery slope effect for euthanasia is taking place in any of the states at the moment. Currently, these figures suggest that fears driven by a slippery slope mentality have not been warranted. Because dying is the most difficult thing any of us will have to face, we need to be particularly sensitive not only to the needs and desires of various patients who are facing such a difficult decision, but we must also honor the decisions made by those whose biases differ from our own.

Common Ground

The main common ground between those who disagree about euthanasia is the value of human life. Those who oppose euthanasia believe in what might be called the sanctity of life. That is to say, life is so valuable that one ought not to end it prematurely. There are often – though not always – religious biases that contribute to this particular view. And these biases might maintain that we are not responsible for our own deaths. God is. And as such, the decision to end our lives is not ours to make. On the other end of the spectrum, for those who support euthanasia, the value of life is so great that one does not see the need for continued suffering during the end-of-life stages. To continue dying in agony makes no sense. To maintain a level of dignity during the process of dying, by having the ability to control how and when one wishes to die, is considered to be of the greatest importance.

Perhaps the greatest common ground between the polarized views regarding euthanasia is *choice*. Can we agree then that liberty and the freedom to choose how it is we wish to die is the common ground on which we can disagree and get along? Would either side really wish to live in a society in which euthanasia was either disallowed entirely or enforced rigorously? For those who do not wish to have medical assistance during the dying process, their choice should be honored. But equally so, would we not wish to extend the same privilege to those who wish for medical assistance in dying? So even though we may disagree about the issue of euthanasia, do we have the intellectual maturity to accept the value of liberty and choice in making such a difficult decision?

(ii) Abortion: Pro-Choice versus Pro-Life

The Extreme Polar Views:

Pro-Life: Never allow an abortion no matter what the circumstances, context, or stage of the pregnancy.

Pro-Choice: Always allow an abortion to proceed if a pregnant woman chooses it at any point in her pregnancy.

This is a very emotionally charged topic that often strictly divides people. Everyone will have their reasons for why they think abortion should or should not be allowed to take place. How well have we thought about why it is that we believe what we do when discussing this particular topic? On which side of the debate do you tend to fall? And why? What would your argument look like? How carefully have you thought about this particular topic? If you believe that an abortion should never be allowed, no matter what the circumstances, what has led you to have this current viewpoint? And conversely, if the decision of an abortion is nobody's business but that of the pregnant woman, what are your premises in support of this view?

At this point I'm going to introduce some conceptual tools that will allow us to better understand where each of us falls in terms of discussing the issue of abortion. The first tool is called the *"Sorities Paradox"*. The word *"sorities"* is Latin for "heap". Imagine that I have bags and bags full of rice, and I intend to create a heap of rice before your eyes. But I am only going to do so by taking a pair of zircon encrusted tweezers and building the heap one grain of rice at a time. As I continue to add grains of rice, and the pile becomes larger and larger, eventually it will reach a size at which you will say that it is a heap. Because we all differ in our views regarding when, exactly, a heap becomes a heap, this demonstrates a shadowy gray area of ambiguity that I call the *"Umbra of Becoming"*. This conceptual tool allows us to better understand states of being as they transition from a state of non-being, to becoming, and then to actually *being*. For example, how many hairs on my head do I have to lose in order to be considered bald? How many pounds do I have to gain in order to become fat? When exactly is a person tall? Or short? Or young? Or old? So the *Sorties Paradox* provides us with a handy metaphor that can be applied to the discussion of the issue of abortion.

And here's how it works.

When it comes to abortion, there are generally three schools of thought: the Conservatives, the Legalists, and the Gradualists. Conservatives believe that life begins when sperm meets egg. After that point, one should not interfere or terminate the fetal process of growth. There are many premises in support of this particular belief. Some are religiously based, others are purely secular. A Legalist, on the other hand, believes that life begins after a fully developed baby exits the mother's birth canal or is removed by Cesarean section. At that point, it is considered alive, and worthy of legal rights as a human being. To a Legalist, the stage of development of the fetus is immaterial, because the woman alone has total control of choice over its continued development or termination. And finally, the Gradualist believes that life begins somewhere between the point of conception and birth. That is to say, for a Gradualist, a fetus becomes gradually *more alive* from the point of conception to the point of birth. With the *Sorites Paradox* and the concept of the *Umbra of Becoming*, you can now better determine how you view the status of a fetus as it moves from a state of non-being, to becoming, to being considered alive and deserving of rights.

It should come as little surprise that there are problems with each particular perspective. To illustrate these, I will use what are called "thought experiments". These are "What if…" scenarios that allow us to more critically consider our currently held beliefs by considering what are called "entailments". The term "entailment" simply means that a conclusion must logically follow a given set of premises. And within each thought experiment, we shall better understand the entailments through the use of the *Sorites Paradox* and the *Umbra of Becoming* as they relate to each of the three perspectives on abortion.

For example, if you are a Conservative, and you believe that life begins at conception, then what this would entail is that, if someone were to stand in front of you holding a petri dish with a frozen sixty-four-celled embryo in one hand and a two-day-old infant in the other hand, and they said that one of those beings was going to die, and they left the choice to you, the choice might not be clear. However, to be consistent in your belief that life begins at conception, you would have to do something similar to flipping a coin. If you chose to save the two-day-old infant, then perhaps you are not entirely a Conservative, because you are admitting to degrees of being. In this case, metaphorically, the two-day-old infant has far more grains of rice than a sixty-four-celled embryo.

If you are a Legalist, and you believe that life and rights begin after the child has exited the birth canal or by Cesarean section, then this logically entails that the mother retains the right to abort the child up and until the point of delivery. In other words, if a few seconds prior to the delivery of the child, the mother asked that the life of the yet-to-be born infant be terminated, this would have to be allowed, since by definition, the Legalist does not believe that the almost-new-born has any rights until it has become separate from the mother. If this makes you feel somewhat uncomfortable, perhaps you are not entirely a Legalist. You too, would be admitting to degrees of being. In this case, according to the Legalist's definition, only a few more grains of rice (another contraction or incision) would have metaphorically made the yet-to-be born infant alive and worthy of receiving legal rights.

And finally, if you are a Gradualist, and believe that life and the rights of a fetus begin somewhere between conception and birth, then this entails that you would know exactly when this takes place. However, this raises the problem of deciding what criteria should be used in making such a determination. Is it the body size of the fetus? A heartbeat? A complete and functioning nervous system? A fetus's reaction to pain? Developed consciousness? There are many criteria to consider. And who is to decide which of these criteria have been satisfied or should be satisfied? If you believe the rights of an unborn fetus should be preserved when it has a fully formed body, with a complete nervous system, then would you approve of an abortion ten seconds (or ten grains of rice) prior to this occurrence? If not, then we need to think more seriously about Gradualism.

The entailment of each one of these positions faces conceptual and practical difficulties. And these difficulties have hopefully been made clearer through the use of the *Sorities Paradox* and the transitional phases of the *Umbra of Becoming*. However, by understanding the complexities and entailments of this issue with greater clarity, and utilizing the six steps, it can become easier to understand why disagreements occur in the first place.

Common Ground

As you can see, in every one of these positions – the Conservative, the Legalist, and the Gradualist – the *Sorties Paradox* and *Umbra of Becoming* demonstrate how difficult it is to make clear determinations regarding the status of the fetus. How many metaphorical grains of rice are necessary to create a heap? Or in the case of abortion, how well have we thought through our particular positions? With such conceptual tools to aid us in better understanding the complexities in discussing these issues, we can go a long way towards understanding how and why we differ in our views about such important issues. Choosing to have an abortion is an extremely difficult decision to be made by any woman. Understanding one another's biases, as well as utilizing conceptual tools like the *Sorties Paradox* and *Umbra of Becoming*, can help us to better understand why it is that we might disagree and how it is that we might agree, in an effort to appreciate such differences of opinion.

And again, the common ground that each side values equally is liberty or freedom of choice. Some are free not to have an abortion, while others are free to do so. Would either side really want to live in a society where the freedom to choose was not available and women were either forced to have abortions or forced to carry out their pregnancies to full term? We may not agree with or like what the other side believes. However, both sides share common ground in regards to the value of choice and the freedom with which to make our own decisions unencumbered by unwanted political pressures.

(iii) Gun Control - For/Against

The Extreme Polar Views:

Pro-Gun: Allow total freedom of weapon possession in the home, in one's vehicle, on a plane, on a train, with a goat, on a boat, on one's person, to be carried while loaded, anywhere and at any time.

Anti-Gun: Collect and destroy all guns and legislate strict laws that have stiff penalties to anyone owning or carrying such a weapon.

Where on the spectrum of this debate do you tend to fall? And why? What would your argument look like? How carefully have you thought about this particular topic? Guns are funny things. They can protect people, provide food and sustenance, or they can terrorize communities and even entire nations. A gun's function is simple: It is a hand-held machine that can immobilize or kill at a distance. Some people love them and just as many hate them. They take lives and they save lives. So how are we to control them? Each country has its own laws regarding the possession and use of firearms. Canadian regulations, for example, are much stricter than those in many of the states in America. And regulations throughout the rest of the countries of the world vary from excessively strict to very lax controls. It would seem that we live in a world where there will always be guns. We cannot get the genie back into the bottle on this one. And so we are torn between simultaneously wanting people to have the liberty and freedom to possess and use firearms in a responsible manner versus the devastating effects that result when they are used improperly.

Common Ground

What appears to be the biggest and most common concern amongst both gun advocates and dissenters alike is the reduction of harm. Most people would agree that when guns are responsibly purchased, licensed, stored, and used, the issue of harm is minimized and we are all on the same common ground regarding rights, freedoms, and liberties. However, accidents happen. And when they happen with guns, people die. And many of those people are children. The Center for Disease Control found that in the U.S., between 2007 and 2011, an average of sixty-two children a year, under the age of 14, were accidentally shot and killed. Many of the children were around the age of 3, and had found handguns (belonging to their parents) improperly secured or stored. The other deaths were by young teens who were playing with the guns, believing they were unloaded. Nobody wants to see children harmed or killed. But is this the price that has to be paid for personal liberty?

A similar case can be made for the accessibility to guns and suicide rates. Those battling mental health issues such as depression, schizophrenia, bipolar disorder, etc., are often faced with the very bleak and hopeless feelings of despair, which they believe can only be resolved by suicide. In these very dark moments, access to handguns provides what appears to be the only solution. According to the CDC, in 2011, in the U.S. alone, there were 42,773 suicide deaths. Half of those suicides were caused by gun infliction. And suicide is the tenth-highest ranked cause of death among all Americans. Whether we disagree on gun policies or not, what we can all agree to is the common ground of reducing harm from gun violence. Let us think very carefully about what we believe in terms of gun control, for the rights and liberties and lives of others are at stake.

(iv) Capital Punishment - For/Against

The Extreme Polar Views:

Pro-Death Penalty: There are specific crimes for which the death penalty is the only just penalty.

Anti-Death Penalty: No matter what the crime, no person should be put to death as a punishment.

On which side of this debate do you tend to fall? And why? What would your argument look like? How carefully have you thought about this particular topic? If you believe that capital punishment should never be allowed, no matter what the circumstances, what has led you to have this current viewpoint? And the same holds for those who believe that people should be executed for specific crimes. Do a Bias Check, and consider the factors that have led you to believe what you now do.

There are several different motivations for punishment, which sharply define and divide specific camps. In the first camp, there is the notion of Retributive Justice: the idea that the punishment should fit the crime. The Retributive Theory states that punishment should be equal to the harm done, either literally an eye for an eye, or more figuratively, which allows for alternative forms of compensation. The Retributive approach tends to be retaliatory and vengeance-oriented.

Another approach is Utilitarian, which maintains that punishment should increase the total amount of happiness in the community. This often involves punishment as a means of reforming criminals, incapacitating or incarcerating them from repeating their crimes, and deterring others. For Utilitarians, the purpose of punishment is to create a better society, not revenge. Punishment serves to deter others from committing crimes, and to prevent the criminal from repeating his crime.

And then there is the Restorative approach. This school of thought believes that there should be a variety of different types of punishments for different types of crimes, but that the ultimate goal for punishment is to balance or restore the harms of the crime to the counter harms of the punishment.

Whichever camp you happen to belong to, it would be beneficial to consider why others might have a differing viewpoint. For those who believe that there are specific crimes worthy of capital punishment, what are those crimes? Should capital punishment only be reserved for the most heinous of crimes? Should specific contexts, acts involving murder, kidnapping, torture, rape, etc., be reserved for the death penalty?

For those who believe capital punishment should never be an option, regardless of the crimes, what are your premises for maintaining this viewpoint? How would you feel if your child was abducted, tortured, raped, and killed? Would you be able to control your baser instincts against the perpetrator for vengeance and harm? Would you be able to accept your own current convictions that no crime deserves the death penalty, when someone you love so much has been treated so horrifically? Or would you want that person put to death for what they have done?

The most difficult aspect of critical thinking is to control our emotions and our passions through reason and fairness. But like the image of the charioteer trying to allow the Facts horse to follow the path of Evidence to Truth while struggling to control the Biases horse which is pulling away from the path, this is not always an easy thing to do. And so we must remember the six steps during the discussion of these extremely emotionally charged issues.

Common Ground

We may not all agree on if or when there should ever be a need for capital punishment. For example, those in favor of it will try to support their premises with statistics that demonstrate how such a punishment deters future crimes. Those against it will cite studies that demonstrate no connection between capital punishment and the deterrence of crime. What we might all agree on is that specific harmful human actions require punishment, both to stop the perpetrator from committing similar acts again, and to let the rest of the public know that such actions are not acceptable and will be punished again in the future. We must make every attempt to keep our biases in check when discussing this particular issue in as fair a light as possible. It is all too easy to get caught up in the emotional rhetoric that underlies the punishment of humans. Again, what we commonly share in our polarized positions on capital punishment is the reduction of harm. Just as with gun violence, innocent people are killed accidentally every year, so too with capital punishment have innocent people been put to their deaths. Is it worth the death of one single innocent person to justify the execution of 1000 guilty others? There are no easy answers. But what we commonly share is that we want what's best for the victims of crime and for society at large.

(v) Same-Sex Relationships – Liberal versus Conservative

The Extreme Polar Views:

Conservative: Sexual education and practice is something to be taught by parents to their children when they have reached the appropriate ages of maturity. Sexual education should not be taught in schools at any age level. Various sexual acts and information are considered to be unacceptable. Same-sex marriage is forbidden.

Liberal: Sexual activity is a natural act. As such, it should be taught in schools at all levels according to the maturity and age of the students. Sexual freedom is tolerated provided that it takes place between consenting adults. There is nothing immoral or illegal about same-sex marriage or same-sex acts.

When it comes to sexual education and practice, how do you define yourself? How liberal or conservative are you? And why do you have the beliefs you now do? What biases throughout your life have led you to this point in time to think about sex the way you now do? For those whose views are more conservative, there is often – though not always – an underlying element of religious belief. For example, the Abrahamic Faiths – specifically fundamentalist Christian views, Orthodox Jewish, as well as Muslim views, place considerable emphasis on controlling one's sexual appetites. Sexual activity occurs between consenting adults – one male and one female. Same-sex activity is considered to be an abomination and therefore is forbidden, and neither practiced, taught, nor tolerated. This has and continues to create considerable difficulty within some religious communities.

Many fundamentalist believers have considerable difficulty accepting that any of their children could be homosexual as opposed to heterosexual. And this is because they believe homosexuality – an act forbidden by God – to be a life choice, an act of free will, and hence, a sin.

Liberals, on the other hand, often maintain that homosexuality is as natural a state as heterosexuality, because it is largely the product of influences that are entirely beyond the person's control. Most Liberals believe that homosexuality is the result of (among other things) biological and prenatal influences. As such, there is no choice or free will involved whatsoever. Therefore, they believe that to hold anyone morally accountable for being homosexual is unfair, unjust, and scientifically indefensible.

Common Ground

It must be extremely difficult for someone with strong religious faith to understand homosexuality in light of their belief system. On the one hand, you have your God telling you that homosexuality is a sin. And on the other hand, your son or daughter turns out to be gay. Trying to reconcile one's supernatural beliefs with the sexuality of one's own offspring cannot be easy. But think of how many people have suffered ridicule, ostracization, torture, and death, just in the past few hundred years, simply for being born with a different set of sexual biases. And yet, to a true believer, to believe that homosexuality is a choice and therefore sinful, worthy of condemning, ostracizing, castigating, and excommunicating a member of their faith, is internally consistent with their entire belief system. Unfortunately, it bears no external consistency to how the world actually functions. There is more than enough evidence, gathered from enough relevant sources, to give a clear indication of the high probability of a natural explanation for homosexuality. This simply makes a true believer's understanding of homosexuality externally inconsistent.

The common ground in this unique case lies in the way in which we accept scientific information. For any true believer, to accept scientific information regarding the successful use of vaccinations, or of the functional use of automobiles, but not to accept it regarding human biological behavior, specifically that of human sexuality, is itself inconsistent. And yet, I genuinely feel for those who have religious convictions that disallow them from understanding the natural state of being that is homosexuality. I know how difficult it must be for them to be faced with the decision between science and their God. And I can appreciate the cognitive dissonance that must result in feeling that they must choose between scientific discoveries and the commands of their God. But this, itself, may be a false dilemma. There are those who resolve the dilemma by considering how God's attributes could allow for homosexual behavior. For example, some maintain that it logically follows that if God created humans, who then developed the science of biology, and the science of biology demonstrates that homosexuality is natural, and what God creates is natural, it must follow – or it entails – that God would not condemn homosexuality. To believe otherwise, would be illogical.

There is also common ground in terms of the love parents have for their children and their desire not to see them harmed. We might want to consider to what extent parents would have to love their children more than their God in order to accept them as homosexuals. But clearly, my current biases influence me to state the conclusion that it is simply wrong to mistreat other human beings for any biological biases beyond their control. Since homosexuality is beyond anyone's control, it follows that it is simply wrong to mistreat people who are homosexual.[29]

And this leads us to a final area of common ground: the reduction of harm. Since we can all agree that people should not be punished for actions they have not committed, or been responsible for, it must follow that it would be harmful to do so. Homosexuality is a state of being that was not chosen and therefore cannot exist as a punishable offense. If any belief system – religious or secular – mistreats or punishes people who happen to be homosexual,

---

29 For the record, this argument satisfies all five of the universal foundational criteria.

the actions must be addressed and stopped. In any society, we want people to have as much freedom as possible. And this includes religious freedom. But whether we are discussing religious freedom or secular freedom, what we would all agree upon as common ground is the understanding that no belief system should be tolerated, if its beliefs generate unwarranted harmful actions to other people or other species.

(vi) God/Religion – Theist versus Atheist

The Extreme Polar Views:

God exists: I know for sure that God exists and that my definition of him is 100 percent accurate and certain. Everyone who disagrees with me is wrong and will be punished eternally in the afterlife.

God does not exist: I know for sure that no Gods exist. Belief in God and organized religions serve absolutely no purpose and should be banished.

Most people in the world (roughly 4 out of 5) believe in some sort of god. And these gods are defined in quite a few different ways, making up over 4000 different types of religions. There are around 1 billion Hindus, 1.6 billion Muslims, and 2.2 billion Christians in the world. Does this mean that any particular god actually exists? Not necessarily. To believe so would commit the Fallacy of Popularity. As we saw earlier, it was once quite popular to believe that the earth was flat and that the sun revolved around it. Popularity alone does not produce truth. It follows then, that it is logically and physically impossible for all the world religions to be correct. However, it is logically and physically possible for them all to be wrong. So why, with so many people in the world believing in various gods, are there some who choose not to believe in any at all?

Atheists state that there is no real convincing evidence for belief in any particular god of any particular religious world-view. They distinguish between knowledge of the natural world and faith in supernatural beings. Knowledge of the natural world is gained through scientific investigation, rational discourse, and empirical understanding. Faith in supernatural beings has no appeal in the natural world and therefore can neither be falsified nor confirmed. Therefore, for atheists, it seems illogical and impractical to believe in things that are beyond empirical investigation.

For theists, however, their sense of spirituality is their greatest joy and produces their strongest set of beliefs. For many theists, their spiritual experiences are deeply personal, emotionally powerful, and not necessarily prone to empirical observation. So how do we disagree and get along?

Common Ground

Just as we saw in the consideration of common ground between Liberals and Conservatives in same-sex relationships, so too do we now find ourselves considering the amount of harm natural versus supernatural beliefs generate. I think both theists and atheists can agree that people should be allowed to believe whatever they want, with the *proviso* that such beliefs do not generate actions that cause harm to other people or other species. We value liberty and freedom of choice, as well as freedom of conscience to believe and practice freely whatever we choose. However, no matter what our views are, it follows that, as a society, we should not have to tolerate unwarranted harmful actions caused by any belief system, whether theist or atheist, secular or religious.

And this leads us to consider another area of common ground between theists and atheists: our shared values. Atheists and theists alike favor many human values and actions such as friendship, loyalty, fidelity, trustworthiness, compassion, honesty, etc. As it turns out, atheists pay their taxes just like theists do. Theists are hard-working, compassionate, and caring people, just as atheists are. Most often, one of the few major differences between the two is a belief in a single god. Other than that, both sides contain people just trying to live their lives in relative peace and comfort. I don't believe theists love their children any less or any more than atheists. And I don't believe atheists care for the homeless any more or any less than theists. People are generally judged by their actions. In the common ground between atheists and theists lie the values that are shared between both world-views, which make it easier to live in disagreement and yet still get along.

Epilogue

The purpose of this book was simple: to provide critical-thinking tools that will allow people to think more clearly and more responsibly – in other words, better – about important issues. It is through the competent and fair use of this skill set that we can better understand how to have intelligent discussions, disagree, and still get along. Though the purpose of the book was simple, our successful use of such skills will require considerable time and practice.[30] But this is to be expected. For critical thinking is not easy. It takes time, and it takes a great deal of effort. But above all, it requires us to embrace the concept of fairness in its application. If we truly value freedom of thought and expression, and the free interplay and exchange of ideas, then we must do so through the continued practice and use of critical-thinking skills. So by all means, let us ride our chariots of impassioned ideas through the streets of discourse; let our opinions and biases clash, but let us also grow thicker skins that will allow us to openly disagree. Over time and through practice, we shall gain greater control to guide the direction of our chariots with the fair use of the *Six Steps to Better Thinking*.

---

30 A final reminder for those interested in pursuing the practical applications of the six steps, please visit: www.sixstepstobetterthinking.com.